SELF-HELP FOR

SELF-HELP FOR YOUR ANXIETY

The Proven 'Anxiety Antidote' Method

ROBERT SHARPE

SOUVENIR PRESS

First published 1979 under the title *The Anxiety Antidote* by
Souvenir Press Ltd, 43 Great Russell Street, London WC1B 3PA
and simultaneously in Canada
Revised edition, with new title, 1991

ISBN 0 285 62986 7

Printed in Great Britain by
The Guernsey Press Co. Ltd,
Guernsey, Channel Islands

Contents

Introduction

YOU *CAN* CONTROL YOUR ANXIETY

Anxiety is a psychological poison which can cause as much distress and, on occasions, do as much damage as a physical toxin.

But there is an antidote. You can learn not only how to control the restricting mental and bodily symptoms of the anxiety response but also how to eliminate sources of fear and damaging stress from your life.

The purpose in writing this book is to train you in the skills needed to exert this control and overcome these difficulties. The procedures taught in the Anxiety Antidote have been developed from the principles of behavioural psychology and make use of the natural mechanisms of the body. These procedures have been successful in helping thousands of people with anxiety problems. They are the most effective long-term answer to a wide range of anxiety-based difficulties and they can help *you* as well, no matter how intense or seemingly complex your current anxieties might be.

If this book is to train you in these procedures as rapidly and effectively as possible, it is important that you follow the training programme as directed. In order to understand how and why the Antidote works at all, it is necessary to possess the basic facts about the anxiety response which you will find in Part One. Each of the skills taught in Part Two evolves from, and builds on, earlier knowledge and practice. The special strategies contained in Part Three will only work efficiently if they are used in conjunction with the procedures described in Part Two.

By going through the programme in the suggested order and by working at the training exercises diligently, you will soon find that the Anxiety Antidote can be made to work for you. The painful mental and physical symptoms of an anxiety attack will be eliminated. You will learn how to replace mental confusion with positive success strategies. You will be shown how to stay calm and perform naturally in situations which currently may cause you excessive anxiety. With the shackles of the handicapping anxiety response finally cast aside, you will be able to let your natural talents and true abilities develop to their full potential.

If you have an anxiety problem, you have probably spent a great deal of time thinking about your difficulties and agonising over the way they spoil your life. Here is your chance to *stop* worrying about anxiety and *start* doing something about it. Work on the training programme now and let the Anxiety Antidote work for you in the future.

Part One

The Anxiety Response

WHY ARE WE ANXIOUS?

If you have ever experienced excessive anxiety, you will not need to be told that the effects are both extremely unpleasant and completely unhelpful. No matter what you are trying to do, the anxiety response ensures that you do it worse! You need to think clearly but your mind is confused by fears. You want to act effectively but your body refuses to obey your commands. As anxiety rises, performance declines, confidence is eroded and ability undermined. However much you may want to defend yourself in a row, rebut criticism, make a good impression, put across your point of view or demonstrate your skills, the anxiety response gets in the way. Your stomach churns uncomfortably, your mouth goes dry, your breathing becomes rapid and uneven, your heart starts to race. You may blush or sweat excessively, tremble or feel dizzy. Your memory fails. Your mind races unproductively. It is hardly surprising that the victim of the anxiety response feels, and frequently looks, ridiculous.

Anxiety can strike anybody at almost any time. As scores of case histories testify, it is no respecter of age, education, social class, intelligence or ability. Take, for example, John, a bright young company executive, who was confident and competent when dealing with any problem at work, but became hopelessly tongue-tied and anxious when he tried to ask an attractive girl for a date. He would blush furiously, stammer hopelessly and feel himself trembling violently.

Anne, another victim of the anxiety response, had been a lecturer at a teacher-training college for six years and enjoyed her work. Then, out of the blue, she suffered a panic attack while talking to a class. 'I suddenly knew I couldn't stand being in the room a moment longer,' she told us. 'I had to get out. I just turned and ran. I have never felt so foolish in my life.'

Mark was an intelligent school leaver who deserved a job with opportunities and promotion. Yet, in the four years after leaving college, he only managed to land menial, dead-end employment. The trouble was that Mark could not handle interviews. He always did well in written tests but went to pieces when it came to direct confrontations with appointment boards: 'I would think out my answers, practice them for days before the interview,' he explained. 'But it never seemed to do any good. As soon as I walked into the room I would forget everything I had rehearsed. My mouth was so dry that I could hardly speak. I could feel myself sweating. I never had a chance to let them see what I was really like.'

One final example will serve to illustrate how widespread and distressing the effects of the anxiety response on a person's lifestyle can be. When she was in her early forties, Susan, the mother of two teenage daughters, developed a fear of leaving the home. This type of anxiety, known as agoraphobia, is a problem which we will deal with in detail later in the book. Susan was deeply ashamed of her fears and did her best to fight them while concealing the truth from her family. As a result, they became bewildered and often irritated by what seemed selfish and eccentric behaviour on her part. Because she was terrified of crossing the road, Susan would take a bus which went half way around the town to get to a point only a few hundred yards from her house. Because it was easier if she drove rather than walked, she would insist on having the family car to travel the half mile to the shops twice a week. Because of her phobia, she turned down all invitations to parties, dances and social evenings organised by her husband's company. To an outsider, Susan appeared to be lazy and antisocial. Only *she* knew the true reason for her actions. 'I was so frightened by what was happening to me that I did not even dare tell my doctor in case he thought I was going mad,' she remembers. 'I kept it all bottled up. The most frightening thing was that I didn't seem to be able to do anything about it.'

This apparent inability to control the effects of anxiety is frequently one of its most distressing symptoms. No matter how often you tell yourself to 'keep calm', 'stay cool' or 'act "naturally" ', you do not calm down, cool off, or begin to act in what you consider a normal manner. In fact, the outcome of such self-exhortations, or the assurances from those around you that 'there is nothing to worry about', is often to increase the level of anxiety. As panic rises, the sufferer finds that he or she is trapped with a rebellious mind in a runaway body.

We all know that it happens. Most of us have first-hand experience of the anxiety response in action.

But *why* does it happen?

What causes these unpleasant and damaging symptoms?

Why is it usually impossible for a person to talk themselves out of the anxiety?

In order to answer these fundamental questions about anxiety, it is necessary to understand the type of mechanisms with which our bodies have been equipped to help us achieve the basic requirement of any successful species – 'survival'.

THE SURVIVAL GAME

We are all programmed for survival. Man is successful as a species because we have learned how to play the survival game better than any other living creatures – at least in the short term. The rules of this game are both harsh and simple. The only thing that matters is winning. The prize is the continuation of the species. The penalty is execution.

The importance of this drive cannot be stressed too strongly, because the way we have been constructed in order to ensure survival is responsible for the anxiety response. We are not talking here about individual survival drives. The fact that thousands of people kill themselves each year and that many more sacrifice themselves for a cause or country each decade does not detract from the argument. These losses, however damaging they are to a particular society or culture, are insignificant compared with the human population of the planet. In a recent book, Dr Richard Dawkins* suggested that the survival game is not really a contest between species but between genes, the building blocks of life. In simple terms, his theory is that the genes, which determine how every part of each animal develops and functions, are blue-prints for survival. This does not imply that they have a 'conscious' determination to endure, but that those which happen to produce a biologically successful species multiply and prosper while those responsible for an unsuccessful biological mechanism eventually disappear. The genes in the dodo which made it slow moving and friendly towards man were backing a loser. The genes which provide the stone fish with its natural camouflage and deadly venom may well be backing a winner.

Imagine that we have been given the power to design a new species. We can give our creatures any physical attributes we wish. The only rule we have to work to is the natural law of survival. What systems should be programmed into our creation in order to give it the best chance of winning the survival game? An examination of past mistakes and failures would indicate that the best design will incorporate three specialised survival mechanisms.

The first is a set of sensors, providing vision, hearing, touch and taste, which will enable the animal to locate food and detect foes as efficiently as possible.

The second are mechanisms which will allow our creature to reach food and fight or flee from sources of danger. There is a wide range of such systems to choose from. We could choose wings, legs or fins. We could settle for claws or sharp teeth. We could design an animal which would run very fast or have an

* *The Selfish Gene*. Dr Richard Dawkins. Oxford University Press.

aggressive nature that made it attack an enemy with determination.

These two systems will have to be connected by the third, vital element in any design. This is a bio-computer, which makes sense of information being fed into it from the environment. It will have to be able to decide which pieces of information mean food and a meal and which indicate an enemy and an attack. The more quickly and reliably this computer can be made to function, the better the chances of survival. A split second of indecision while information is being processed could mean the difference between escape and death. On the other hand, it will be very wasteful, and potentially damaging, to have the computer running at maximum speed the whole time. If our creature responds with hair-trigger sensitivity to every possible threat, it will constantly be jumping at shadows or striking out in wasteful attacks. So much energy will be burned up and so little time will be used productively in replacing what has been lost, that it is likely to perish through exhaustion. If we slow down the reactions too much, of course, it will soon become the victim of a rival with faster responses.

This problem can be overcome if we give the computer two circuits. The first is used for coping with normal situations, the second will be brought into action when an emergency occurs. This should, in theory, provide our species with the best of all possible worlds.

These three systems can be found in all higher forms of animal life on earth. But they never all develop to the same level in a particular species, since some will be favoured at the expense of others. Compared with many species, our sensory systems are primitive. We cannot see, hear or taste as well as most wild animals. A dog has a better sense of smell than its owner, a cat more acute sight and sharper hearing, a pigeon a better sense of direction than most humans. At our strongest, we are puny compared with many animals the same size as us or larger. We cannot run as quickly, jump as far, leap as high, dive as deeply or escape from danger as efficiently as many of our rivals in the survival game. Yet, despite these seemingly devastating handicaps, we are not only ahead of the field but we have even found out how to manipulate the rules of the game to our advantage.

This has only been possible because man has followed the unique evolutionary path in developing a bio-computer at the expense of the other systems. Thanks to this enormously complex and versatile mechanism, our species has flourished. But this sophisticated and imperfectly understood computer is also the prime cause of our anxiety difficulties.

ANXIETY AND THE AUTONOMIC NERVOUS SYSTEM

When describing how the bio-computer might work most effectively to ensure survival, it was suggested that it would be valuable to have two different circuits. The first could be used at normal times when there was no threat to survival; the second, more sensitive, circuit would automatically come into operation as soon as a threat was perceived.

The human brain and central nervous system, which links it to every part of the body in a circuit carrying two-way traffic of information to the brain and instructions from it, work along these general lines. Within the central nervous system there are two distinct pathways linking areas of the brain in charge of different functions. A part of the brain known as the *cerebral cortex* is responsible for intellectual skills. A second system, controlled by a part of the brain called the *hypothalamus*, looks after the routine tasks involved in keeping us alive and acts as an automatic alarm system.

As you read these words both systems are in operation, enabling you to understand what is being said and keeping you alive and well while doing so. The 'thinking' part of the brain, the *cerebral cortex*, is sorting out the signals from your eyes and, by reference to the memory banks, deciphering the symbols which make up these words. While these and other intellectual tasks are being performed, the network of nerves regulated by the *hypothalamus* is supervising the routine bodily functions necessary to sustain life. Without your having to 'think' about it, your heart pumps blood with a regular beat of between 60 and 90 contractions a minute. Your lungs expand and deflate due to signals sent automatically to the muscles in your chest and diaphragm. If you have recently eaten a meal, the food is being digested without any intellectual intervention on your part.

Because these and many other physiological activities essential to life are carried out automatically, the nervous system responsible for them is termed the *autonomic nervous system* (a.n.s.). Most of the time it is more than merely convenient that this system is able to work independently of the *cerebral cortex*. If we were only able to remain alive by constant attention to the mechanical processes of the body, life would rapidly become impossible. Imagine having to remember to *order* your heart to beat every second of the day and night or dying of suffocation because you became distracted and forgot to tell your chest to expand and contract!

But having a part of the nervous system which is, for most practical purposes, beyond the control of the 'thinking' part of the brain does have some disadvantages as well. It means that when the *autonomic nervous system* becomes super-active, no amount of positive direction from the *cerebral cortex* is going to calm things down. You can assure yourself that there is no danger, no cause for the racing heart and churning stomach. You can order your body to slow down and relax. But there are no effective lines of command between the *cerebral cortex* and the *autonomic nervous system*, so the soothing messages either fail to get through or are ignored. As a result the *cerebral cortex* can itself become aroused and confused.

We can liken the situation to a ship which is steaming across calm, safe waters when it is suddenly caught by an unexpected storm. The danger soon passes and the captain, realising that there is no risk to his vessel, prepares to steam uneventfully onwards. But down in the engine room there is panic. Some of the crew remember that, after a similar squall a few weeks earlier, their ship got into real difficulties. In a frantic effort to escape from what they assume to be a dangerous situation, they start to stoke up the boilers and switch off the regulators. The captain is astonished by this quite unnecessary response and signals for a slow down in operations. But the crew take no notice of his urgent signals, some are misunderstood, some fail to get through and others are merely ignored in the confusion below decks. Those that are received often make matters worse. Acting on the belief that: 'If you can keep your head while all around you are losing theirs, you can't have the slightest idea of what is going on!' the crew assume that their captain is either blind or incompetent. They continue to run full speed ahead. After a time, even the captain begins to accept there must have been a mistake on his part. 'Perhaps I have got the situation wrong,' he thinks frantically. 'All this panic below decks must be caused by something. What does my crew know that I don't? My God this is frightful, we *are* going out of control!'

Matters are made worse when another section of the crew attempts to return the ship to normal running. They start to shut down the boilers and close the throttles. Other crew members fight for the controls in order to put the vessel back into emergency running. The panic below decks spreads throughout the ship. The loss of control is complete.

In this nautical analogy, the *cerebral cortex* is the captain, the *autonomic nervous system* the crew. Those who were responsible for sounding the alarm and stoking up the boilers in the first place belong to a part of the *a.n.s.* known as the *sympathetic* branch. The crew members who attempted to cool down the situation and bring things back under control belonged to a different portion of the same *a.n.s.* called the *parasympathetic* branch. These two branches of the *a.n.s.* are mutually antagonistic, a fact that enables them, under normal circumstances, to regulate one another.

The *sympathetic* branch is energy expending. Like an eager extravert, it is always 'raring to get up and go'. The orders it gives to the body are 'speed up' commands: 'Beat faster heart

. . . more respiration . . . more sweating.' The *parasympathetic* branch is energy conserving. Like a cautious older brother, it works hard to check the excesses of its impetuous companion. When the *sympathetic* branch tries to increase heart rate and respiration, the *parasympathetic* branch orders a slow down.

When the *sympathetic* branch diverts blood to the arms and legs, for reasons which will become clear in a moment, it is the *parasympathetic* branch which restores the flow to normal running. The branches of the *a.n.s.* can be compared to the two ends of a seesaw. When one comes up the other goes down. Most of the time a balance is sustained.

A threat to survival will dramatically upset this balance in favour of the *sympathetic* branch, because the second main function of the *a.n.s.* is to help us escape from hazardous situations. It does this by switching the body over into an emergency running mode which offers the best chance to do battle or to run away. For this reason, the *a.n.s.* is often referred to as 'the fight or flight' mechanism.

As soon as a danger is perceived, the *sympathetic* branch takes command. It steps up the heart rate and speed of respiration to ensure that large quantities of well oxygenated blood reach the brain, arms and legs. Additional blood supplies are diverted to these parts of the body from the skin and digestive tract. Digestion is slowed down. There is no point in wasting resources in processing food if, as a result, survival is put at risk. Glucose is released from the liver to provide energy for the muscles. The sweat glands are instructed to work harder because perspiration will help to cool down the body during the burst of vigorous activity which is expected to follow. There are many other more subtle changes as well. For example, the speed with which blood clots is increased so as to minimise the effects of injuries.

If there really is a major, physical threat to survival, then the actions of the *sympathetic* branch have been highly desirable. The mind is alert, the limb muscles primed for action and all inessential mechanisms have been temporarily closed down. When 'the fight or the flight' are concluded, the *parasympathetic* branch will have little difficulty in restoring the systems to normal running order.

The heart rate and respiration will be slowed down. Blood pressure will fall and the blood will be returned to the skin and digestive tract. Digestion will start up again. Sweating will be reduced. The emergency systems will have performed in a perfectly logical, reasonable and efficient manner. The chances of survival will have been greatly enhanced.

But suppose that the *a.n.s.* has made a mistake? There is no *real* danger, no genuine threat to survival. It makes no difference to the initial surge of *sympathetic* arousal. Adrenalin is released, from the adrenal glands located above the kidneys, and carried by the bloodstream to all parts of the body. It is important that this should happen without any intervention by the 'thinking part of the brain' because any pause for an objective consideration of the threat could put survival at risk. A Stone Age hunter hearing a noise in the undergrowth had to react instantly to the slightest possibility of danger. If he had carried on a debate with himself about whether that was the *particular* kind of noise made by an enraged sabre-toothed tiger or wind rustling the leaves his lifespan would probably have been even shorter than it already was. He needed that unthinking, instant trigger which set in motion all the beneficial changes of autonomic arousal.

But if there *is* no danger; if the *a.n.s.* has sounded off like a faulty intruder alarm for no good reason, what subsequently follows will seem both illogical and alarming to the person involved.

The stomach churns following the first spurt of adrenalin. The heart begins to beat more rapidly and the rate of respiration increases. The person starts to sweat and may go pale as blood is diverted away from the skin. At this point the 'thinking' brain often takes over. It demands to know just what is happening! Reason dictates that there is no survival threat – so why all the panic?

'Pull yourself together,' commands the *cerebral cortex*. 'There is no need for all this tension. You are only going to stand up and talk to a group of your colleagues, or have a discussion with your spouse, or make love to an attractive partner, or go out shopping. Where is the threat or danger in that?'

But, as we have seen, the *a.n.s.* is not under the direct control of the *cerebral cortex*, so none of these logical and soothing arguments has the slightest chance of reducing the level of arousal. In fact, they may have quite the opposite effect. When there is no reduction in the anxiety symptoms, the person may start thinking: 'Oh my God, I've lost control. I *am* going to panic and make a fool of myself.' The physical confusion feeding back to the *cerebral cortex* confirms such negative thoughts. These statements of impotence and panic are, in turn, detected by the body and increase the level of arousal still further.

When nothing actually happens to justify the emergency measures which the *sympathetic* branch has taken, the *parasympathetic* branch starts to restore order. It begins to reduce heart rate and steady the breathing. It restarts digestion and diverts the blood back to the skin surface. The *sympathetic* branch, which is still getting highly arousing messages from the panic-stricken brain, refuses to accept that there is no survival threat. It speeds up the heart again, increases respiration, changes the flow of blood back to the muscles and brain, and halts digestion.

The effects of this battle between the opposing branches of the *a.n.s.* are traumatic. The heart thumps wildly. Breathing is rapid and unsteady making it difficult to talk clearly. The face may become deathly pale and then blush bright scarlet. The stomach will churn and may cramp painfully. Muscles which are tensed and then relaxed by the conflicting orders often start to tremble violently. Extra blood being directed to the brain and then withdrawn again can lead to a feeling of giddiness and a fear of fainting. Increased sweating will make the palms damp and soak the clothing. In a major panic attack, relaxation of the muscles controlling the anal sphincter and the bladder may lead to even more embarrassing soiling. The mouth will go dry as the production of saliva is halted. There may be a feeling of nausea caused by the stop-start orders given to the digestive tract.

As these physiological changes are monitored by the *cerebral cortex*, mental confusion is very likely to develop. So much attention is being focused on the way the body is behaving and on negative thoughts about one's inability to control these responses, that memory and concentration are seriously impaired. The bio-computer is being swamped with confusing and contradictory messages. What is termed a panic spiral may develop. It ends with the victim of the anxiety attack being unable to move or help themselves in any way. 'I crouched in a doorway for over an hour too terrified to move,' an agoraphobic reported.

Other anxiety sufferers respond to this kind of internal assault by fleeing from the situation no matter what the cost. A public speaking phobic described how he literally raced from the meeting he had been supposed to address. 'My whole career depended on that presentation,' he recalled. 'All the directors were waiting to hear my views. I was a hundred per cent confident in my material. I knew it could have been the triumph of my life. But all I wanted to do was get the hell out of it . . . so I did.'

Not everybody experiences anxiety in this very physical way. Some people respond mentally without displaying any obvious signs of the turmoil going on inside. They may feel their hearts beating rather more quickly than usual, their stomachs might churn uncomfortably, they may sweat a little more. But mostly the panic is confined to their minds. It is a tumult of conflicting and confusing thoughts: 'I cannot cope!', 'I must escape!', 'I am going to faint!', 'I cannot stay here any longer!', 'I am going to make a fool of myself!'

A person suffering from this sort of anxiety response can appear to be perfectly at ease. There will be few outward signs of the inner chaos and these will probably only be noticeable to a trained observer. But the victim may be so panic-stricken that he or she will be looking without really seeing, listening without hearing, moving without knowing where they are going or why. The *sympathetic* branch of their *a.n.s.* has been aroused and is causing them to respond in a quite inappropriate way to a situation which offers no objective threat to survival.

Let us now define anxiety in a way which incorporates the facts we have so far discussed. We know that the response results from bodily changes triggered by some situation which is considered, rightly or wrongly, to put our survival at risk. We can, therefore, consider anxiety as:

An Individual's Mental and Physical Response to a Survival Threat

Restating anxiety in these terms means that we can regard it as a natural and logical bodily response rather than in abstract and intangible psychoanalytical terms. If this definition is correct, it should be possible to:

(1) Locate various anxiety symptoms in different parts of the body and thinking processes.
(2) Measure their effects using scientific equipment.

Both these things are, in fact, possible. We *can* identify, locate and measure the different elements of the anxiety response as accurately and objectively as we can measure blood pressure and monitor heart beat. Anxiety need no longer be regarded as some strange and mysterious force welling inexplicably from deep in the subconscious mind. It has a reality which can be discussed and dealt with in physical terms.

A second advantage which this sort of definition has over vague, subjective descriptions is that it identifies the response as arising from a *survival threat*. Since survival is the most important goal of any species, it is quite reasonable for us to respond rapidly and intensely when any such threat arises.

But, of course, the response occurs in a vast number of situations where there is no objective danger. It is reasonable to assume that a hunter tracking a wounded beast to its lair will benefit from the bodily changes triggered by the *sympathetic* branch of the *a.n.s.* It is much less obvious why a spider phobic should experience the same intense response when confronted by a harmless, if hairy, house spider. A front line soldier under fire is correct in assessing his situation as hazardous to survival. But why should somebody who is having a row with the boss, waiting to be interviewed, trying to make a date or going out to a party suffer from the same level of autonomic arousal?

The answer turns out to be devastatingly simple. We become anxious in situations which do not offer any objective threat to survival because we have *learned* to respond in this way.

HOW WE LEARN TO BECOME ANXIOUS

It is possible to define three major types of anxiety which can affect us in almost every area of life. These are:

(1) Objectively real threats.
(2) Subjectively assessed threats (phobias).
(3) Threats to expectations and self-image.

In each of these, learning plays an important part in the intensity and effects of the anxiety response. Let us look at each of them in turn to see how they arise.

1. Objectively Real Threats

You are walking at night down a lonely street. Suddenly a man armed with a cosh jumps from an alley and comes menacingly towards you. Your first reaction, although you may not notice it, will be the startle response. This will be experienced as a lurching sensation in the pit of the stomach as the first spurt of adrenalin arrives. In a fraction of a second, your whole body will have been switched into the 'fight or flight' mode. Whatever happens in the next few minutes, autonomic arousal *should* ensure that you have the best chance of surviving. If you decide to run from the attacker, your limbs will be well supplied with glucose and oxygen-rich blood, providing the energy sources needed for vigorous action. People who have escaped from hazardous situations often reflect with astonishment at their enormous strength, speed and agility: 'I seemed to have the power of ten men,' commented a slight young schoolmaster who lowered children to safety from a burning hotel. Your mind should be super-alert, enabling you to think much more swiftly and clearly than under normal circumstances. A girl who struggled safely ashore after her car plunged 30 feet to the bottom of a harbour recalled how calm she had felt as she sank with her vehicle: 'After a moment of intense fear my brain cleared. It was like watching everything in slow motion. Except that I was doing everything very rapidly. I opened the window to equalise the pressure, unclipped the catch, opened the door and swam up to the surface. I felt totally in control.'

In these situations, and at this level of arousal, the functioning of the *a.n.s.* is valuable and adaptive. It is aiding survival. After the danger has passed, the *parasympathetic* branch is able to restore the body to normal running quickly and easily.

The arousal will be damaging and dangerous, however, if it spirals out of control. Then the mind will become panic-stricken and confused, leading to ineffective and possibly fatally wrong decisions being taken. 'Many fire victims would have lived through their ordeal if they had remained calm,' fire experts frequently comment. What they really mean is 'if the victims had been able to control their level of justified autonomic arousal'.

The two methods by which arousal under hazardous conditions is normally kept in check are discipline and training. Soldiers, police officers, fire-fighters and emergency rescue workers and others in high risk occupations not only train thoroughly so that they know almost by instinct what to do in the real situation, but they also subject themselves to rigorous discipline. In combination, these provide a very effective means of controlling autonomic arousal. The soldiers of the First World War marched in an unbroken line to certain death because their tough drill had conditioned them to unthinking obedience. The modern soldier is expected to be much more of an individual, but the basic concept of regulating anxiety by disciplined training remains.

Anybody who wants to take up a risky sport, such as flying light aircraft, skin-diving, parachuting or mountain climbing must voluntarily subject themselves to equally disciplined training if they are to survive. Even then panic can break through, especially in the early days of training. Flying instructors, for example, can usually recall a number of students who froze behind the controls, their eyes unseeing, their limbs set in almost catatonic rigidity as the aircraft plunged earthwards. Many mountaineers have stories to tell about the terrified novices who become immobile half-way up a sheer rock face.

If you intend to perform any high risk activity, then you should certainly train under expert guidance and keep your skills fresh by constant practice. Even then, there may be occasions when the anxiety level *does* start to rise in response to an unexpected and novel hazard. In these circumstances, the Anxiety Antidote, plus thorough training, will greatly improve your chances of coming through unscathed.

The Antidote will also help you cope effectively with those emergencies for which prior training is almost impossible: the criminal attack, the hotel fire, the automobile crash or the household accident. Staying calm and acting sensibly in any of these situations can help to minimise injury or damage and might help to save your life.

2. Subjectively Assessed Threats (Phobias)

A phobia (the word is derived from the Greek for 'fearing') is considered to be an 'irrational fear' because no objective threat is involved. The level of anxiety in these situations is often very high and this fact, plus the illogical nature of the response, leads many phobics to believe that they must be going crazy. Frequently, they are so ashamed of their problem that they go to great lengths to hide it even from close relatives. Susan, whose case we mentioned earlier, is an example of a phobic who was too embarrassed even to mention her difficulties. If you have a phobia let me start by offering these assurances. However restricting, intense and irrational the response may be, it is not a symptom of madness. Secondly, it is seldom realised that you can become phobic about anything and everything on earth. The most commonly discussed phobias are those centred around crowded places (agoraphobia – 'a fear of the market place') confined spaces (claustrophobia), flying, dogs, spiders, thunder storms and eating in restaurants. But there are also many thousands of people who are phobic about travelling on public transport, insects, earthworms, blood, hair, vomit, bridges and birds.

In order to understand how such apparently incomprehensible responses can arise, it is necessary to look at the way in which we acquire fresh knowledge and new ways of behaving. When we talk about 'learning', most people tend to think in terms of formal education, of mastering new skills or the ability to play a game or sport. In fact, almost everything which we can do, with the exception of certain reflex responses, is a result of learning. We relate to people, hold political and religious opinions, initiate conversations, assess the merits or otherwise of new acquaintances, make love, money and new friends, well or badly, correctly or incorrectly as a result of the ways in which we have *learned* to do so. In my book *The Success Factor*,* I described how it is possible to learn the habit of success and pointed out that the majority of people who fail do so because they have learned the habit of failure. Phobias develop for just the same reason: as a result of inappropriate learning.

If we repeat any activity often enough, we will eventually

* *The Success Factor – How To Be Who You Want To Be.* Souvenir Press Ltd.

come to perform it so easily that it may not require any conscious thought. If you can ride a bicycle or drive a car, consider how straightforward it was when you first learned the skill.

Reinforcing Learned Behaviour

In order to speed up the learning process and sustain motivation, it is helpful to introduce a system of rewards. Some activities such as eating, making love and playing a sport are rewarding in themselves. Other less attractive and stimulating behaviours may require external rewards to establish them. For example, if six-year-old John sets the table for lunch and gets a hug from his mother, he will be more likely to set the table again. If he is hugged *immediately* after he has set the table, he is more likely to associate the pleasant response from his mother with the table setting behaviour. If she says nothing at the time but gives him an affectionate hug the following day, then he may not associate setting tables with being hugged. In this case, the reward will have very little effect on the frequency with which he sets the table.

In behavioural psychology, these rewards are called *reinforcers*. Research has given scientific proof of what common sense suggests in the first place. The more immediately a piece of behaviour is followed with a reinforcer, the more firmly and quickly that piece of behaviour will be established. The greater the delay between a piece of behaviour and a reinforcer, the less effect it will have on establishing behaviour.

There are two types of reinforcer. The first is a reward, such as praise, the show of affection, or the payment of money. These are known as *positive reinforcers*.

The second involves the removal of something unpleasant. This is called a *negative reinforcer*. If a child is crying but stops when her mother makes a fuss of her, then the child will have been *positively reinforced* for the crying behaviour. The mother will have been *negatively reinforced* by the child ceasing to cry.

It is this process of *negative reinforcement* which is very largely responsible for a phobic response becoming established in the first place. Once it has occurred, it may be sustained by both *negative* and *positive reinforcement*.

Two examples, drawn from case histories, should help to explain how this happens. Joy is in her late forties and suffered from a phobia which made it impossible for her to drink out of cups or glasses. She could only sip liquids out of a spoon or saucer. This may sound like a very odd kind of anxiety problem but it is not all that uncommon and it is extremely restricting. Joy was unable to accept invitations to cocktail parties or to dine out. She was embarrassed about inviting friends to eat at her home. She would not eat in public and gave up a job she enjoyed because the morning coffee break made her so anxious.

Joy, like the majority of phobics, could remember how her problem started. 'I was on holiday and staying in an expensive hotel. At dinner one evening I sipped a glass of wine while talking and swallowed the wrong way. I had done this sort of thing before but this was especially painful. I thought I was going to choke to death. I made a terrible fool of myself. Everybody in the room turned to see what was happening. My throat was painful all that night. When tea arrived next morning I picked up the cup and found my hand was trembling so violently I could not hold it. I left my tea untouched. At breakfast, I had the same reaction when I reached for the coffee cup. I felt excessively anxious. The thought was hammering away in my mind that it would all happen again. So I went without coffee that morning and felt relieved. I found that I could drink without intense anxiety only if I sipped the liquid from a bowl or a very shallow cup. But soon even that became impossible.'

Joy's phobia developed very quickly. Alec, a dog phobic, found that his fears grew gradually over a period of months. They began when he saw a dog fight in the street outside his house: 'I had my seven-year-old son with me at the time and so I was possibly more anxious than I would have been on my own.

I hurried the boy across the street and we went into a shop until the animals had been pulled apart by their owners. A few days later I was walking to work when I saw a large, black alsatian without a collar pacing down the street towards me. I felt extremely anxious and went into a shop until it had gone past. The following afternoon I was travelling by bus when a woman got on holding a poodle. She sat beside me and I felt my heart start to pound. I began to feel sick. The dog's head was level with my face and although it looked quite friendly I was convinced it would bite me, perhaps blind me. I got off the bus and walked home.'

At the end of six months, Alec was experiencing excessive anxiety even in the presence of a playful puppy. The sight of a dog a hundred yards away made him feel extremely nervous and upset. He started to avoid going out and eventually moved from the suburbs to the inner city. He disliked his new surroundings but felt that they were less dangerous because he encountered far fewer dogs.

Although they seem at first sight to be very different, these case histories have much in common. Both Joy and Alec experienced an initial spurt of anxiety following moderately traumatic incidents. Their response was to avoid similar pieces of behaviour in the future. Joy would not drink out of a cup, Alec went out of his way to avoid dogs. These escape and avoidance responses provided strong *negative reinforcement*. When Joy took the decision not to attempt to drink her cup of morning tea, and when Alec was able to dodge inside a shop to get away from the alsatian, they both experienced a great wave of relief. They had escaped from unpleasant situations. The tremendous feelings of relief they then felt rewarded the behaviour very powerfully. After a time, a very short time in Joy's case, this new piece of learning had been firmly established. The mere thought of having to drink out of a cup or face up to a dog generated anxiety. Avoidance and escape strategies produced pleasant sensations of relief. As these pieces of behaviour became the norm, the level of anxiety experienced in the presence of the phobic stimulus rose and the symptoms grew more intense.

Why should some people develop a phobia as a result of a mildly frightening encounter while others will be able to dismiss the incident from their minds easily? There is no simple answer. It may be that some people are biologically more vulnerable than others. Also, periods of great mental or physical stress, such as following a bereavement or after a difficult birth, may make a person more open to a phobic attack than at other times. There is also some evidence from research that women are at greater risk during the four days prior to their menstrual period. Illness can reduce a person's resistance and increase the possibility of a phobia developing if some traumatic incident takes place during this critical time.

A recent survey suggested that as many as 83 per cent of phobics were able to remember the episode which started their phobic difficulties. Both Joy and Alec could give very clear descriptions of the incidents surrounding the birth of their phobia. But such insights are not an essential ingredient of the treatment. The Anxiety Antidote like any effective treatment does not depend for its effectiveness on knowing where and when a person was first exposed to the attack.

Let us pause now and take stock of the points we have covered so far. They are important and you will find it helpful in the training programme which follows to have an understanding of the ways in which autonomic arousal takes place.

We have seen that arousal to situations which are actually hazardous is both sensible and adaptive. It helps us to survive. We have also seen how it is possible for the body to learn to respond with sympathetic arousal to a very wide range of stimuli which are not objectively hazardous. It could be argued that dogs can cause injuries, diners occasionally choke to death, cars and buses do crash, people are sometimes killed by lightning, not all aircraft reach their destinations safely and so on. But these are not really sound reasons for being phobic about dogs, cups, transport, thunder storms or flying because the level of risk is extremely small. The chances of survival are heavily in favour of the individual. None of these arguments can help the phobic, of course, because they are intellectual rationalisation and, as such, the property of the *cerebral cortex*. It is enough for the *sympathetic* branch of the *a.n.s.* that they have come to be *perceived and assessed* as a survival threat. Once this has happened, the automatic response of the *sympathetic* branch is to key up the body for 'fight or flight'. It is this switch from normal to emergency running which the sufferer experiences as anxiety symptoms.

3. Threats to Expectations and Self-Image

A recent survey produced the following list of anxiety problems:

ANXIETY CAUSED BY:
chances of promotion
playing a game of golf
position in class
letting parents down
husband's lack of affection
threat of nuclear war
not having as smart a home as my sister
trying to ask a girl for a date
lack of physical attraction
fear of making a fool of myself in public
making love
visiting parents-in-law
negotiating deals
criticism from employers
size of penis
wondering what the neighbours think of me

None of these, not even the spectre of a third world war, can realistically be described as posing an objective threat to survival. A phobic difficulty could have explained some of them, but this was not suggested by the terms in which the anxieties were expressed.

Yet each of these situations was generating a high level of anxiety. The *sympathetic* branch of the *a.n.s.* was responding as though they threatened the individual's survival. In a sense they did. But what was being placed at risk was not biological survival but something which was largely the creation of their own thinking processes – their expectations and self-image.

All men share the same biological survival needs of oxygen, food and water, protection from structural damage and an environment which offers a fairly narrow range of ambient temperature. As Kipling expressed it: 'The Colonel's Lady and Judy O'Grady are sisters under their skins.'

But the Colonel's Lady and Judy O'Grady, despite their biological similarities, had very different self-images and expectations. These were shaped not by the needs of physical survival but as a result of the accident of birth, social class, education, prospects, abilities and attainments.

To some extent, factors beyond our control have a role in shaping our self-image and expectations. Whether we are considered handsome or beautiful, plain or downright ugly will depend not merely on what we actually look like but on the culture into which we are born. A woman considered attractive and desirable by a Samoan or Arab male would probably be regarded as unpleasantly plump by most European men. A beautifully slender American model might be ridiculed as a skinny freak in parts of Africa. Beauty is in the eye of the beholder and the beholder has been conditioned by the culture in which he or she lives.

But the fact that it stems from a highly subjective social judgement does not diminish the significance of good looks in determining expectations and self-image. Research in the United States has shown that people assessed as 'attractive' are less likely to be found guilty by juries and more likely to receive light sentences if they are convicted than people considered as 'unattractive'. Other investigations have suggested that 'beautiful people' can expect better service in restaurants, more consideration in times of difficulty and a greater chance of promotion at work.

Gender is another important factor beyond our control. Here again cultural attitudes and social judgements play an important role. The self-image and expectations of an educated woman living in New York or London will be very different from those of a submissive Japanese or Arabian housewife. Expectations are also shaped, to some extent, by the activity of the glands which control the body's metabolic rate and level of aggression. You can transform an apathetic and lethargic individual into a bustling go-getter by injecting the right hormones. You can calm down an aggressive person or change a mild individual into a violent one with equal ease. Here again, factors which are largely beyond our control are involved in creating a particular set of expectations and determining self-image.

But no less significant is the part played by individual learning and social conditioning. In primitive or impoverished societies, expectations mainly focus on basic survival needs and anxieties will revolve around such essentials as sufficient rain, healthy cattle and abundance of crops.

The expectations of a prosperous middle-class couple in the Western culture are liable to be a long way removed from such fundamental survival needs for very obvious reasons. Their physical survival is never normally in such jeopardy. Food is readily available from the local stores, water may be obtained at the turn of a tap, their household environments can be adjusted at will, thanks to central heating and air conditioning. Their expectations are much more likely to focus on job prospects, pay rises, and achievements at work or in the community. Anything which threatens these expectations can cause them as much anxiety as a prolonged drought, sickly cattle or a crop failure will cause to the impoverished farmer.

This comparison may strike you as both absurd and offensive. A poverty stricken peasant facing starvation and an over-fed executive passed by for promotion hardly seem to be confronting equally serious survival threats. One is staring death in the face, the other merely may not be able to change his car this year as planned. How can these situations be equated?

However odious it may seem, the comparison is physiologically valid. Anxiety occurs as a result of sympathetic arousal. This arousal takes place in response to a survival threat. As we saw in the case of the subjectively assessed phobic threat such arousal does not depend on the reality of the threat. It is enough to *believe* that a threat exists for the person to become highly aroused and extremely fearful. It is the same with expectations and self-image. Although these are very largely subjective concepts which we have created for our own benefit, any attack on them can prove as frightening as a threat to our physical survival.

Expectations can be either positive or negative and so can the components which make up self-image. The higher and more positive our expectations, the stronger and more positive our self-image is likely to be. A business executive who *expects* to land multi-million pound contracts, who *expects* to manage a multi-national company before the age of forty, who *expects* to get the best possible deal out of any negotiations, is likely to have a self-image which includes confidence, drive, assertiveness, intelligence, commercial acumen, intuition, determination, courage and cunning. A high court judge who *expects* to deal fairly with all who come before him and *expects* to be able to hand out justice without fear or favour, is likely to have a self-image which includes concepts of integrity, intellect, judgement, perception and scrupulous fair-mindedness. On the other hand, a person who has failed in a number of businesses and has a record of broken marriages is more likely to have a self-image as unlucky, badly treated, insufficiently intelligent, under confident, incompetent and any of the other negative attributes commonly attached to a lack of success in life.

It is very often impossible to determine which comes first, the expectation or the self-image. Is a person confident because he expects to be confident or does he expect to appear confident because he feels himself to be a confident person? So far as this programme is concerned, the debate is unimportant. All that you need to bear in mind is that this type of anxiety can arise as a result of any of four situations:

(1) A situation which *places a high level positive expectation* in jeopardy. The more important the expectation and the more serious the threat, the greater the likely anxiety.

(2) A situation which *casts doubt on self-image*. The greater the importance which is attached to that element of self-image, the greater the likely anxiety.

(3) Any pieces of behaviour which *are assessed as being unhelpful* may be a source of anxiety because, by definition they threaten expectations or self-image. The more negatively the piece of behaviour is assessed the greater the anxiety it is likely to generate.

(4) Any *negative expectation will automatically produce a certain amount of anxiety*. Such anxiety is most likely to be described by the sufferer as a type of depression. It arises as a result of inadequate reinforcers being present in the person's lifestyle. The solution, as I shall demonstrate in Part Three, is to inject an increasing number of reinforcers and positive pay-offs into the lifestyle. The difficulty is that this type of anxiety reduces motivation for change. This is an important aspect of anxiety and one to which I shall return in Part Three.

The following lists show the nine major areas of expectation and the nine basic aspects of self-image in terms of positive and negative elements. Needless to say, these lists are far from exhaustive and you will probably be able to think of several more, either positive or negative, from your own experiences.

1. Expectations

Expectations	May Include	
	Positive	Negative
What we expect *from* ourselves.	High standards of intellect. Skill. Determination. Loyalty. Tolerance. Honesty. Courage, etc.	Low levels of intellect. Lack of skills. Lack of determination. No firm loyalties. Lack of tolerance. Dishonesty. Cowardice, etc.
What we expect *for* ourselves from life in general.	Reward for effort. Respect. Recognition. Fair dealing. Rights as individual. Consideration, etc.	To be cheated. To be regarded as inferior. To be misunderstood. To be treated with indifference. To be downtrodden, etc.
What we expect *from* intimate relationships.	Love. Affection. Honesty. Tenderness. Discretion. Sex. Co-operation. Comfort, etc.	Exploitation. Indifference. Harshness. Abuse. Aggression. To be cheated. To be hurt, etc.
What we expect *from* our children.	Obedience. Love. Respect. Regard. Consideration. Admiration. Support. Success, etc.	Disobedience. Contempt. Lack of respect. Scorn. Failure. Abuse. Lack of concern. Indifference, etc.
What we expect *from* our close relatives.	Affection. Patience. Understanding. Loyalty, etc.	Scorn. Contempt. Indifference. Lack of understanding. Disloyalty, etc.

| Expectations | May Include | |
	Positive	Negative
What we expect *from* our friends.	Loyalty. Friendship. Co-operation. Sympathy. Honesty. Respect. To be assisted in times of difficulty, etc.	To be let down. To be lied to. Indifference. Lack of respect. To be exploited, etc.
What we expect *from* peer groups.	Co-operation. Honest treatment. Recognition of our skills. Respect. Sharing of workload, etc.	To be exploited. To be looked down on. To be disliked. To be cheated. To be made a fool of, etc.
What we expect *from* our subordinates.	Respect. Obedience. Loyalty. Honesty. Hard work. Co-operation. Admiration, etc.	To be disliked. To be cheated. To be disobeyed. To be put upon. Not to be admired or respected, etc.
What we expect *from* our superiors.	Recognition for our skill and effort. Fair dealing. Understanding of our needs and wishes. Patience. Consultation. Respect for our standing in firm. Reward for work, etc.	To be exploited. To be regarded as inferior. To be disliked. To be hard done by. To be cheated. To be down-trodden. To be abused. To be criticised. To be treated with contempt. Not to be adequately rewarded for effort, etc.

All these expectations, both positive and negative, greatly influence self-image. In turn, self-image affects our expectations. In general, the more positive the expectations the more positive are the self-image components. The more negative the expectations the more negative the self-image. But it is a chicken and egg situation and very often it is impossible to say whether negative expectations are sustaining the negative self-image or the other way about.

2. Self-image

Self-Image General	May See Self As	
	Positive	Negative
Self in relation to self.	Achieving desired goals. Being fulfilled. Having clear set of principles to guide one. Getting places in life. Making use of skills. Likeable and attractive. Virile. Good looking. Perceptive. A success, etc.	Failing to achieve potential. Not finding fulfilment. Drifting. A disappointment to oneself. Shackled by lifestyle. Unattractive to others. Ugly. Insensitive. A failure, etc.
Self in relation to world in general.	Ambitious. Assertive. Patient. Intelligent. Skilled. Capable. Friendly. Important. Influential. Practical, etc.	Unambitious. Under-assertive. Dull. Unskilled. Incapable. Unsociable. Insignificant. Powerless. Impractical, etc.
Self in relation to intimate partners.	More loving. More dominant. More tolerant. Equals. More competent. More intelligent. More sexual. Equally sexual. Honest, etc.	Inferior. Not emotionally involved. Intolerant. Less competent. Less intelligent. Less sexual. Less honest, etc.

Self-Image General	May See Self As	
	Positive	Negative
Self in relation to children.	Loving. Easy going. More important. Equally important. Generous. Deserving of love and respect. Affectionate. Patient, etc.	Indifferent. Harsh. Less important. Mean. Not worthy of respect or admiration. Unable to show emotions. Impatient, etc.
Self in relation to close relatives.	More important. Equally important. More intelligent. Equally intelligent, etc.	Inferior. Less capable. Less important. Less intelligent, etc.
Self in relation to friends.	More important. More capable. Equally important or capable. More intelligent or wealthy. Equally intelligent or wealthy. Superior socially. Equal socially, etc.	Less important. Less capable. Less intelligent. Poorer. Socially inferior, etc.
Self in relation to peer groups.	More important. Equally important. Superior in some way. Equals in all respects. Deserving of loyalty. Deserving of respect. Deserving of fair treatment, etc.	Less important. Inferior in some way. Unequal in some respects. Not deserving loyalty. Not worthy of respect. Not likely to be treated fairly, etc.

Self-Image General	May See Self As	
	Positive	*Negative*
Self in relation to subordinates.	More important. Equally important. More skilled. Equally skilled. More intelligent. Equally intelligent. Worthy of respect. Not threatened by their abilities and ambitions. More ambitious. Better liked by superiors, etc.	Less important. Less skilled. Not so intelligent. Not worthy of their respect. Disliked. Threatened by them. Less ambitious than they are. Less hard working. Less liked by superiors, etc.
Self in relation to superiors.	Respected. Trusted. Well liked. Superior. Equals. Luckier. Harder working. Their social equals, etc.	Not respected. Not trusted. Inferior. Disliked. Lazier. More cunning. Their social inferiors. Unluckier. Fearful, etc.

ANALYSING EXPECTATIONS AND SELF-IMAGE

It is sometimes very helpful to sort out exactly what expectations you have in life and to examine your self-image in terms of positive and negative components. Where there is generalised anxiety which does not seem to relate to any specific situation, such an analysis will sometimes bring to light current sources of anxiety and, in addition, help to pinpoint possible areas of difficulty in the future.

In order to illustrate how this can be done, let us look at two case histories in which the people concerned were initially unable to identify particular problems as these outlines of their difficulties indicate.

George, a 32-year-old computer designer, married with two sons, aged nine and six, described his problem as follows: 'Recently things have been getting on top of me. I am constantly on edge and terrified for the future. The fears are vague. I have not any special worries at the moment but I dread waking up in the morning. I do not have any particular physical symptoms although I have noticed that I sweat a lot more these days than I used to. I have no appetite either. My stomach is always upset. Mostly it is mental confusion. I cannot seem to concentrate on my job. At home everything builds up and up to a point where I can only cope by going for long walks on my own. My wife really does not understand and feels that I am being weak.'

Mary, 28, worked in a junior position in an office before marrying at the age of 19. She has twin boys aged eight and works part-time as a typist. 'I can remember when it first happened. I was washing some clothes about two years ago when suddenly I became overwhelmed with panic. There was no reason why this should have happened. I just froze in the kitchen. My heart was racing and I was panting. My hands were shaking and I thought I was going to faint. I felt terribly sick and giddy. My palms were soaked with sweat. Since then I have felt generally nervous. I cannot seem to relax. Every so often for absolutely no reason, I get these terrible panic fits. My doctor put me on tranquillisers but they only helped a little and I hate taking drugs. I hate the idea of depending on them.'

The first stage in the analysis is to obtain detailed information about their lives in relation to the nine Expectation and Self-Image categories. In the descriptions that follow, the information has been changed in minor details to protect the identity of the subjects. The transcribed tape recordings have been edited in order to make them easier to follow.

George

1. Expectations

WHAT HE EXPECTS FROM HIMSELF

> 'I am intelligent and have been trained to a high level of skill of which I am justly proud. I am honest when dealing with my friends and loyal towards people who trust me.'

WHAT HE EXPECTS FOR HIMSELF FROM LIFE IN GENERAL

> 'I believe that hard work and effort should be recognised. I want to be treated as an individual not as a number on a pay envelope.'

WHAT HE EXPECTS FROM INTIMATE RELATIONSHIPS (WIFE AND CHILDREN)

> 'I expect my wife and children to show me the same love that I feel for them. I think that children should be obedient to their parents and respect them. I want my children to be honest and to tell the truth. I have ambitions for them. I want them to work hard at school and obtain good grades so that they can earn enough money to live well.'

WHAT HE EXPECTS FROM HIS FRIENDS

> 'I look for companionship in my friends. I want to be able to share my ideas and plans with them and talk things over.'

WHAT HE EXPECTS FROM HIS COLLEAGUES

'At work I expect my colleagues to support me in my efforts and do as much work as I do. I want them to accept that I have a skill and recognise my ability in areas where I have special expertise.'

WHAT HE EXPECTS FROM HIS SUBORDINATES

'I expect subordinates to do what I tell them and to respect my judgement on topics which I have been trained to understand.'

WHAT HE EXPECTS FROM HIS SUPERIORS

'I want my boss to realise I am a skilled person and an individual. As such he should respect my views or at least take note of them. I want a fair return for my skills and efforts. If changes have to be made then I want to be consulted.'

2. Self-image

SELF IN RELATION TO SELF

'I feel that I have made the most of my abilities and chances in life. I have no religious belief but I am guided by moral principles. I would not cheat a friend or hurt anybody unnecessarily. I am not worried about the way I look. I do not have any hang ups about virility. I know that I am no great lover but I certainly get by in that respect. I regard myself as successful.'

SELF IN RELATION TO WORLD IN GENERAL

'I am ambitious but probably not assertive enough in making my demands known. I am confident about my work but less certain in many social situations. I think I am rather withdrawn.'

SELF IN RELATION TO INTIMATE PARTNERS

'With my wife I am rather submissive, I suppose. Anything for a quiet life. She is much more practical than I am in anything which does not involve work. She plans our holidays, for example, and takes the major decisions about the children.'

SELF IN RELATION TO CHILDREN

'I hope that my children will work hard because I want them to achieve more than I have. I am fairly easy going most of the time but when I put my foot down I am, perhaps, a bit harsh. I am worried that they do not respect me sufficiently.'

SELF IN RELATION TO CLOSE RELATIVES

'I regard myself as rather superior to my own father. He was never as ambitious as I am and didn't achieve much in life. My wife's parents come from a rather better class of society than I did. Her father is a bank manager. I feel somewhat reticent in his presence.'

SELF IN RELATION TO FRIENDS

'I regard myself as friendly and sociable although I only have one or two close friends. My best friend I have known from school. I regard him as extremely successful, more so than I am. He is also very intelligent. I suppose that I am slightly flattered by the fact that he finds me good company.'

SELF IN RELATION TO COLLEAGUES

'I am loyal to my colleagues. I would always support them if I thought they were in the right. I am not sure how far I would go, however, if there was real trouble. I don't think that I would put my job at risk for the sake of a colleague. I am not sure about that. It would depend on circumstances.'

SELF IN RELATION TO SUBORDINATES

'I believe that people junior to me in the office do respect me. I try to be fair with them at all times. But if I say something must be done in a certain way I expect them to do it without argument or discussion because I am more experienced than they are.'

SELF IN RELATION TO SUPERIORS

'I regard myself as equal to my boss. We are both skilled in different ways. I do not see myself as inferior to him in any way. He respects my judgement in my area of expertise and I respect his managerial skills.'

Mary

1. Expectations

WHAT SHE EXPECTS FROM HERSELF

> 'I was never very bright at school. I always seemed to be at the bottom of the class. But I am clever at practical things. I think I am a good mother because I have a lot of patience.'

WHAT SHE EXPECTS FOR HERSELF FROM LIFE IN GENERAL

> 'I want to be left alone to get on with my life. I wouldn't want to push myself into the limelight. I like a quiet life with my family. I try to be pleasant to everybody.'

WHAT SHE EXPECTS FROM INTIMATE RELATIONSHIPS

> 'I want my husband to be affectionate and support me in decisions about the children. I expect him to be honest and always tell me the truth. I believe I deserve that because I am truthful with him. I think a husband and wife should be completely loyal to one another. I would support him even if I thought he was in the wrong.'

WHAT SHE EXPECTS FROM HER CHILDREN

> 'I expect my children to love me because I love them. I want them to be honest with me and never lie. I think they are both much more intelligent than I was.'

WHAT SHE EXPECTS FROM CLOSE RELATIVES

> 'I want my relatives to understand my difficulties and help me. I think that families should stick together.'

WHAT SHE EXPECTS FROM HER FRIENDS

'I would never break faith with a friend. I would stick with them through thick and thin. I expect them to do the same for me. I hate malicious gossip and never say anything unkind about people behind their backs. If they have something to say I prefer them to say it to my face.'

WHAT SHE EXPECTS FROM HER COLLEAGUES

'I want people I work with to be fair with me, not to say something critical behind my back. I expect them to do their fair share of the work and not push it onto me. I want them to like me.'

WHAT SHE EXPECTS FROM HER SUBORDINATES

'I don't like office juniors to be cheeky. I think they should have some respect for people older than themselves. I was always very respectful of my seniors when I was a child.'

WHAT SHE EXPECTS FROM HER SUPERIORS

'I want to be thanked if I do a piece of work well or if I stay behind to finish up a rush job. I expect my superiors to remember their place and not try to take advantage. Some bosses think it OK to take liberties. I have left several jobs because of this. They should be courteous and not take advantage of a woman.'

2. Self-image

SELF IN RELATION TO SELF

'I am quite happy with what I have achieved in life. I never thought of myself as very bright and I had no ambitions for a career. I just wanted to marry and have children. I think I am very affectionate and loving. I look attractive and take care to keep my looks. I feel I owe this to my husband. I am a Roman Catholic and the faith helps me. I try to live according to my beliefs.'

SELF IN RELATION TO WORLD IN GENERAL

'I am not as clever as my husband or children but I do have a lot of love to give. I am patient so long as people are honest with me and do their best. I love my home and keeping it clean and tidy. I like to have everything in its place. Perhaps I am rather too houseproud but I hate mess.'

SELF IN RELATION TO INTIMATE PARTNERS

'I always do what my husband wants provided it does not concern the children, I only stand up to him over them. We occasionally argue about them but I know I am right in wanting the best for them. In other ways I am very willing to accept what he says. I am attractive and enjoy sex with my husband now and again but not as a matter of routine. I am a truthful person and never try to hide my feelings from him.'

SELF IN RELATION TO CHILDREN

> 'I believe I am a good mother. At least I hope so. I try very hard. I am very proud of my children. I want to admire them and I do.'

SELF IN RELATION TO FRIENDS

> 'I am not a very sociable person and dislike parties. When I do go I prefer to find a quiet corner and stay there. I do not like mingling with strangers.'

As you can see, not all the Expectation and Self-Image headings were considered relevant by the subjects. George, being more work-orientated, found it easier to state his expectations and describe his self-image in terms of career and professional success. Mary was much more concerned with her family and home life.

Having extracted this type of information, it is possible to produce lists of Expectations and Self-Image attributes and then grade them according to their importance to you.

Expectations

First, a positive hierarchy list is prepared, containing all those aspects of the two categories which are regarded as beneficial. Some people find it helpful to give them a numerical value. Although this marking is obviously a very subjective assessment, it does help to provide a basis for evaluating and comparing different expectations.

Using a numbering system, each expectation can be rated at between 0–10. Those which are considered important and necessary to achieve will receive between 6–10 points. Those which are regarded as relatively less important or less likely to be achieved are given from 1–5 points. Expectations which are not seen as especially important are zero rated. When going through the examples below, remember that each judgement is a subjective one relating only to the lifestyle of the individual concerned.

Example One

HIGH RATED EXPECTATIONS (Score +6 to +10)
I expect to receive promotion (+8).
I expect my wife to be faithful to me (+9).
I expect to have a regular sex life (+9).

Example Two

LOW RATED EXPECTATIONS (Score +1 to +5)
I expect to be treated fairly by my boss (+5).
I expect to remain loyal to my firm (+4).
I expect never to be let down by my friends (+3).

Example Three

ZERO RATED EXPECTATIONS
I expect to remain healthy.
I expect to be friendly with my neighbours.
I expect never to be criticised.

These illustrate the kind of expectations which one man might have. Another would probably assess them totally differently. Somebody who considered friendship extremely important would perhaps rate the expectation of loyalty from friends much more highly but be less interested in promotion at work. A health fanatic might be very concerned with staying healthy but much less concerned with enjoying a regular sex life.

If you have any difficulties in evaluating any of your own expectations, imagine a situation in which a particular expectation is suddenly dashed, by an accident, illness, change of circumstance or bad luck. How would you take the blow? Would you consider your life empty and meaningless from then on or would you be able to recover quickly from the loss? Would you merely think – 'That's how it goes' or might you feel shattered and devoid of hope?

So far we have only considered positive expectations. But you may have listed some very negative ones. You could be anticipating failure in business or in your private life. You might expect *not* to be able to achieve promotion, make friends, enjoy a relaxed sex life or sort out marriage difficulties. To place a numerical value on this type of expectation, ask yourself how likely the prediction is to come true and how badly you would feel about it should the worst happen. The higher the probability of the expectation being fulfilled and the greater the anxiety this produces, the higher the negative score.

Example Four
HIGH RATED NEGATIVE EXPECTATIONS (Score −6 to −10)
I expect to fail in business like my father (−9).
I expect to finish up in a mental hospital like my brother (−10).
I expect to remain housebound for the rest of my life (−9).

Example Five
LOW RATED NEGATIVE EXPECTATIONS (Score −1 to −5)
I expect to have a row with my wife almost every day (−3).
I expect that my children will disobey me (−4).
I expect that I will be let down by my partners (−5).

Example Six
ZERO RATED NEGATIVE EXPECTATIONS
I expect to catch a cold this winter.
I expect my children will occasionally disobey me.
I expect that I will never become company chairman.

Here again, the grading of negative expectations is a completely subjective matter that will vary drastically from person to person.

Self-Image

In order to list the components of self-image you must look at your major positive expectations and answer the following question: 'Is the way in which I behave in order to achieve that expectation harmful to my chances of success?'

As with expectations, these pieces of behaviour can be given either a positive or negative value. Using the 0–10 points system, a piece of behaviour assessed as being extremely helpful might be given a value of +10 while a very unhelpful piece of behaviour might be rated as −10. For example, a business executive who expected to achieve a high position in his company (a +8 expectation) might assess his loyalty and hard work as being helpful to his chances (+8 and +9) while his lack of self-confidence and inability to express himself clearly were very damaging to prospect of promotion (−6 and −8).

To illustrate this point let us compare the Expectation and Self-Image lists prepared by George and Mary.

George

EXPECTATION	IMPORTANCE
To stay on top of my job and obtain the financial rewards due to me	+10
To be respected and admired by my colleagues at work	+9
To be regarded as fair and honest in all my dealings	+9
To be loved by my wife and children	+8
For my children to be successful and happy	+8
To receive the support of my colleagues	+7
To be respected by subordinates	+7
To be liked by those I work with	+6

By answering the question: *'Is the way I behave helpful or harmful to my chances of success?'* George discovered that he regarded himself as intelligent (+8), ambitious (+8) and confident at work (+8), as honest (+7) and loyal to colleagues (+7). But he also saw himself as socially inferior to his father-in-law (−5) and too strict with his children (−4), he felt that he was too subservient to his wife's views (−6) and lacked confidence in handling social situations (−6). He regarded his physical appearance as being neither important nor detrimental to any of his ambitions. It was given a zero rating.

Mary

EXPECTATION	IMPORTANCE
To be regarded as a good mother and wife	+10
To be loved by my children	+10
To be loved and protected by my husband	+10
To be told the truth by my husband and children	+9
To have my children grow up healthy and normal	+9
To have loyalty from my husband	+9
To be understood by my relatives	+7
For my children to be successes	+7
To be respected by people I work for	+6

Mary's self-image analysis showed that she regarded her qualities of love and caring to be extremely important in realising her major expectations (+9), she also saw herself as practical (+8) and proud of her family (+8). She rated her sexuality less highly (+4) but thought that her attractive physical appearance did help her keep the love of her husband (+5). She felt that it was important for her to be understanding towards her family (+8) and honest in her dealings with others (+6). She did not regard herself as very intelligent and felt that this was a handicap (−2) but not a very serious one. She felt that she was lacking in assertion at work but again, since her working life was relatively unimportant to her, this did not seem especially detrimental to her expectations (−3). She would have been much more concerned about a lack of assertion when dealing with her children but she did not consider that this was a failing she possessed.

WHAT THE ANALYSIS TELLS US

The advantage of using a numerical score system over straight description is that it enables us to get an immediate idea of areas where both expectation and self-image are the strongest. One almost always finds where expectations are high, self-image will also be high. This is because one reinforces and strengthens the other. Success in attaining important sub-goals on the road to overall success – or the realisation of the expectation – favours those pieces of behaviour which produced it. For example, suppose a man finds that with hard work and application he rises quickly in his company. Each promotion will make him more certain than ever that he is right to favour these tactics as a means of realising his financial and commercial expectations. Another individual in the same company has found that cheating and flattering are just as good as the less palatable alternative of work and worry. So he proceeds to use them in his climb to power. Each time they achieve him a promotion or some other goal, he will be reinforced in his view that they are the best methods to use. By carrying out your own analysis along these lines, you should be able to identify those expectations and the different components of self-image most likely to produce anxiety, whether positive or negative.

You can then start to combat current anxieties and take preventive measures against possible future sources of anxiety in three ways:

(1) Use the Anxiety Antidote taught in the next part of the book to control the anxiety response.
(2) Use the special Antidote strategies contained in Part Three to overcome any negative self-image components which are currently preventing important expectations from being realised.
(3) Reassess your expectations and self-image to see if you are being realistic. Have you set yourself impossibly difficult goals? Are you being too optimistic about your current level of abilities, or too pessimistic about your skills? Have you based your expectations on reliable information or on pious hope? An occasional stock-taking of one's expectations and self-image can do a lot to eliminate unnecessary anxieties. This does not mean you should underestimate your talents or accept second best. It *does* mean that you should examine exactly why you want to achieve a certain goal. 'All my working life I had wanted to be a chief librarian,' a middle-aged woman told us. 'Each time vacancies occurred I would work myself into a fever of anxiety. Should I apply? Would it mean too many changes? Would I stand a chance? Sometimes I did go after the job but I was never successful and the failure made me bitter and miserable for weeks afterwards. Then, one day, after an unsuccessful interview, I stopped and thought hard about my ambition. Why did I want the job? I was perfectly happy where I was. I enjoyed the work I did, I liked the people I worked

with. I did not need the money or especially want the additional responsibility. The only reason I had gone after the job was that I had convinced myself I should have the position. Two years after I stopped trying I was appointed chief librarian at my own branch on the retirement of the previous chief.'

Let us now look at George and Mary to see how their analysis helped resolve the anxiety difficulties which had caused both so much distress.

George

At work both his expectations and self-image are high. There seems to be no threat to either at this stage of his life, although these are vulnerable areas simply because he has such strong expectations and such positive self-image. Situations which could produce anxiety difficulties in the future will include anything which puts in jeopardy his expectations or threatens that self-image. For example, he would probably be extremely anxious if he felt that an error of judgement on his part had called into question his intelligence or abilities. He might feel anxious, although slightly less so, if somebody accused him of petty dishonesty. If a subordinate whom he regarded as less able and industrious was promoted over his head this, too, could lead to high levels of anxiety because it would threaten his expectations that hard work, effort and intelligence were the pathways to promotion.

Since the work situation was generally favourable it seemed clear that the threat responsible for his anxieties must be sought elsewhere. At home, he had a moderately high level of expectation coupled with a very negative self-image. This was a much more likely source of the anxiety. As he had high positive expectations for his children, he was asked to consider if they could be causing him anxiety. George agreed that his elder boy was a source of worry to him. He had recently transferred to a new school and his reports, which had previously been good, were now poor. He was getting lazy and seemed indifferent to his studies. George blamed his wife for not putting more pressure on the boy to work harder. This had led to rows between them which he had lost. He felt that his inability to stand up to his wife and to make his views known and acted on was harming the boy. He feared that the child would become a failure and that this would be his father's fault. In discussions with his son, the boy often made use of his mother's arguments to support his attitude towards school work. 'He would tell me his mother said it was crazy to spend nice evenings indoors studying. That he should be out playing like the other boys. I felt unable to answer him effectively because I knew that I always gave in to her.'

George's problems were resolved in two main ways. First of all, he was trained in the *Antidote* procedures which enabled him to bring his anxiety response under control. Then he was shown how to assert himself in discussions with his wife. She came to realise that his point of view was just as valid as hers and that they should discuss matters and take joint decisions rather than leave everything to her. Far from harming their relationship, this new approach actually improved their marriage. Secondly, George was shown how to set more realistic goals for his children. He was helped to realise that they were individuals in their own rights, not surrogates who had to achieve his personal goals and ambitions in life.

George's behaviour was modified, with his co-operation and approval, so that his self-image was raised in the family situation and his expectations were made slightly more realistic. He also saw where anxiety difficulties might arise in the future, especially in relation to his work. This enabled him to take stock of his expectations and approach life in a more relaxed manner. He became far more approachable and this increased his popularity at work. A few months after he came to see me he was, in fact, passed over for promotion when a nephew of the managing director was appointed to a position which George, along with everybody else in his department, expected to go to him. 'If this had happened to me a year ago I think I would have quit,' he told me. 'It was so contrary to everything I had expected from the company. It was unfair and unjust. I got anxious but successfully used the Antidote procedures to bring down the level of anxiety. When I was calm, I applied the strategies I had been taught and saw the situation in its true perspective.'

With the pressure off him, the older boy improved at his school work and began to enjoy a much better relationship with both his parents. 'I used to expect admiration and respect from my children simply because I was their father,' says George. 'Now I realise that you only get admiration and respect from people if you do things to deserve them.'

Mary

As we saw, Mary's anxiety difficulties struck her down like a thunderbolt. One moment she was, apparently, a happy and well adjusted woman. The next instant she had become panic-stricken. This is by no means a rare occurrence. A graphic description of such a panic attack is given by Henry James Snr, father of the famous novelist, in his book *Society, the Redeemed Form of Man*. James had just finished dinner and was sitting alone in the room watching the dying embers of the fire. He was feeling content and relaxed after an excellent meal: 'When suddenly, in a lightning flash as it were, – "fear came upon me, and trembling made all my bones to shake". To all appearances it was a perfectly insane and abject terror without ostensible cause . . . the thing had not lasted ten seconds before I felt myself a wreck, that is reduced from a state of firm, vigorous, joyful manhood to one of almost helpless infancy.' He goes on to describe how he remained seated in the dining-room, not daring to move or call for help, until he had recovered his composure. 'This purpose I held to for a good hour . . . beat upon meanwhile by an ever-growing tempest of doubt, anxiety and despair. . . .'

Why should such an unexpected and distressing respons occur without any prior warning?

Mary's analysis suggested that worries about her work wer unlikely to be at the basis of her difficulties. Although he self-image was not very high in this area, neither were he expectations. She had no career ambitions, and was quit prepared to change jobs if they didn't suit her.

At home, she had a high expectation score and an even highe self-image. At first sight, it seemed improbable that she could t suffering anxiety as a result of some problem in this life area Her expectations were quite realistic. She knew that she was capable mother who cared for her family well and loved the very deeply. Clearly, however, anything which threatened he expectations or self-image in this life area would produc anxiety. We saw, in the case of George, that where there is high level of expectation and self-image, the individual potentially vulnerable to attack. If Mary had any reason t suppose that her husband was having an affair or that he children had stopped loving her, she would certainly fe extremely anxious. She would also become anxious if anyor cast doubts on her abilities as a wife and mother. But none these things had happened.

At first, Mary was unable to think of any incident whic might explain excessive anxiety concerning her family. Severa days after she had carried out the analysis, however, somethin did occur to her which might possibly have been responsible fc her sudden rush of fear. 'I had read a magazine article about schoolgirl called April Fabb who left home to cycle to a friend house. She never arrived. She just vanished into thin ai Nobody ever saw her again. I remember thinking what he parents must have gone through and how her mother must hav felt. I tried to think what I would have done in her place. Ho I could have coped.'

Mary had no recollection that she had been thinking abou this particular story just prior to her first anxiety attack. Bu there was no need for her to have done so. The onset of fea

THE ANXIETY RESPONSE 59

could have been triggered by a sudden thought that the same tragic fate might overtake her own children, or her husband.

Mary's whole life was bound up with her husband and children. She hardly existed as an individual in her own right. I am not saying that this was necessarily undesirable but it did make her especially open to anxieties concerning her family. 'I realised that all my worst fears were centred on my husband and children. If he went out by car I used to worry frantically that he would be injured or killed in an accident. I never let the girls go to school on their own, even though other parents let children of that age do so. I worried when they were away in case something happened to them. I wouldn't let my boy go to summer camp with the school because I thought it would be too dangerous. I was only really happy when they were all at home and under my wing.'

As with George, Mary was shown how to use the *Anxiety Antidote* procedures to bring her mental and physical responses under control. She was then helped to develop a more realistic attitude towards the risks of everyday life. She was encouraged to find interests outside her home so that she could get family life into a clearer perspective. After a few months her problems had been resolved.

In these cases, analysis was helpful in identifying anxiety sources and suggesting vulnerable areas where anxiety might strike in the future. But I must make it clear that in carrying out such an analysis I am not adopting a psycho-analytical approach. Insights into basic behavioural problems, such as an inability to assert oneself effectively or to accept the hazards of daily life in a realistic manner are helpful only in so far as they suggest suitable training procedures.

Finally, it must be made quite clear that one does not have to understand exactly how and why a particular anxiety problem has arisen in order to use the Antidote. One of the great advantages of the procedures is that they can be applied to all types of anxiety, however they are caused. If you can gain further insights into your problems by carrying out a behavioural analysis, however, it will help you to use the appropriate strategies which are taught in Part Three of this book.

ANXIETY AND LIFESTYLE

In real life, the clear-cut distinctions we have made between the three major sources of anxiety seldom exist because so much overlapping takes place. What starts as a specific anxiety response can easily generalise into a major phobic response. This, in turn, will alter our expectations and self-image, usually for the worse, and so introduce further sources of anxiety.

There are four stages by which this usually happens:

Stage One – Startle
An incident produces a startle response. This is frequently a perfectly logical and adaptive reaction to a situation which has an objective element of risk attached to it.

Stage Two – Avoidance
Later a similar situation is avoided because memories of the earlier incident generate anxiety. This response makes it harder to confront the situation in the future.

Stage Three – Lifestyle Changes
In order to avoid further confrontations, the lifestyle is changed, often drastically. These restrictions on behaviour can lead to frustration and depression.

Stage Four – Expectation and Self-Image Adjustments

As the lifestyle changes expectations and self-image are also adjusted to include the need for avoidance. Negative expectations and a lowering of self-image result in generalised anxiety. This further affects performance and limits the range of options available. After a time, the original incident may have been forgotten but the widespread anxiety of which it was the seed is now flourishing.

These four stages are well illustrated in the case of Phyllis, a 22-year-old secretary. Until she was 18 Phyllis enjoyed socialising. She went to a great many parties and found it easy and pleasurable to make new friends.

Her difficulties began when she went to a friend's birthday party soon after a bad bout of the 'flu. Although she was fully recovered, Phyllis was run down and somewhat depressed as a result of the illness. That evening a rather aggressive man with too many drinks under his belt made a pass at her. When she refused, he became insulting and a fight developed between her escort and the man. Normally, she might have dismissed the episode as a joke. But now it began to prey on her mind. She had felt anxious during the confrontation and afterwards, when she thought about what had happened, she experienced the same high level of anxiety. Stage One of her anxiety problem had been completed.

A few days later she was asked to another party. Memories of the incident were still fresh in her mind and the anxiety that a similar thing might happen again made her back out of the invitation at the last minute. 'When I phoned up just before the party was going to start and said I had a bad headache I felt very relieved,' Phyllis recalls. Stage Two of her anxiety problem was now taking place. Other invitations in the next weeks were also turned down. After a time her friends stopped sending them. They did not like to be constantly rejected.

Because she felt embarrassed, Phyllis began to change her lifestyle. She stopped seeing many of her old friends, took on extra work at the office so that she had a reason for not going out at night. She grew increasingly lonely. Her life became a long, dreary routine of work, more work and the isolation of her apartment. After a time, Phyllis came to believe that she actually preferred to live this kind of existence, even though it left her depressed and frustrated. Fortunately, she met a man at the office who fell in love with her and refused to accept her excuses. He also helped her overcome her anxieties by encouraging her to seek professional help from a behavioural psychologist.

When she looks back on those years of fear and misery, Phyllis, like many former anxiety sufferers wonders how she survived. One woman, who had endured restricting and painful anxiety responses for more than ten years, described the moment when she took the first positive steps back to a normal life like this: 'It was like being allowed out of gaol.'

If you too have been imprisoned by your anxieties, hopefully you now know how and why sentence was passed in the first place.

In Part Two you will find the key of the gaolhouse door. Beyond lies freedom.

Part Two

The Anxiety Antidote

INTRODUCTION TO THE TRAINING PROGRAMME

To be able to use the Anxiety Antidote, it is necessary to learn four basic skills:

(1) Relaxation and Correct Breathing.
(2) Sleep Protection.
(3) Positive Self-Talk.
(4) Anxiety Management.

These can be used together with the special strategies contained in Part Three. You will find it quite easy to master the skills and put the strategies to work for you by following the training instructions.

The skills which are being taught in this programme have previously only been generally available under professional guidance in a consulting room setting. They are powerful, behavioural procedures which should be taken seriously or left alone.

Children and the Anxiety Antidote

If your main interest is in helping children with anxiety problems, then we advise you to read the modified Relaxation and Anxiety Management programmes, which we have included at the end of the two adult sections. You should also take special note of the Antidote strategies contained under the 'Family and Children' section in Part Three.

Even if your main concern is anxiety in your children, you are first advised to learn the Antidote yourself and start working on any of the appropriate strategies in Part Three. There are several reasons why you will be able to help your children most effectively if you, and ideally your spouse as well, are also following the training programme.

First of all, anxiety difficulties in children are frequently a reflection of a high level of anxiety within the family unit or a result of anxiety difficulties in one of the partners. It is much harder for children to overcome their own problems if this situation remains unchanged. Very often, a lowering of family tension proves a prime factor in the reduction of childhood anxieties. Indeed, simply by eliminating general stresses within the group, you may remove a specific difficulty in the child.

The second advantage of the whole family learning the Antidote is that children respond very readily to the example of their parents. If the child sees that you are taking the training seriously, then he or she will be much more likely to become involved in the programme.

Finally, by following your own course of training you will be able to understand how the skills work in practice, rather than simply in theory. In this way, you should be able to provide the most effective support and guidance for the young child.

Any child from the age of about five upwards can benefit from learning the Antidote. Indeed, at this age, and for a few years after, the child already possesses the first essential skill – that of being able to relax quickly and easily. It is only through experiencing the tension of life that this vital ability is gradually lost. If we were able to institute just one change in the educational system of the West, it would be to train every child in the Antidote. In this way, they would grow up knowing how to control their own bodies and regulate their responses to stress in the most effective and reliable way possible. An enormous number of anxiety-related difficulties, which now arise in childhood, at puberty and during adolescence, could be avoided and the youngster could grow into a confident, anxiety-free adult. Sadly, it is unlikely that any country will be far-sighted enough to introduce such a training course as part of the normal academic timetable. But this is no reason why individuals should not include the Antidote in their own approach to child rearing. Most responsible parents safeguard their children against the risk of drowning by teaching them how to swim as early as possible. Teaching them how to survive the anxieties of life is no less important.

Drugs and the Anxiety Antidote

If you are taking a course of prescribed drugs, such as Valium or Librium, you should *not* discontinue the treatment when starting this training programme. Even after you have mastered the skills and find that you can control your anxiety symptoms very effectively without the use of tranquillisers, you should only stop taking them on the advice of your doctor. Consult the practitioner who prescribed the drugs in the first place. Explain that you have learned how to use the natural mechanisms of the body to bring your anxiety responses under control. They will probably suggest that you either stop taking the drugs or that you gradually phase them out of your life. This is often the preferred system, since it allows you to get used to a new method of anxiety control gradually.

How to Use the Training Programme

Each of the three skills starts with a description of how and why it works. This is followed by detailed training instructions. At the end of each section you will find a summary which includes the key points to be carried out when mastering that skill. This can be used for quick reference and will avoid the need to read the whole set of instructions when actually carrying out the training. But go through the complete training method a number of times so that you completely understand what is involved at each stage of the programme. Do not try to start a fresh piece of training until you are confident in your ability with the earlier skill. As we explained in our introduction to this book, the skills evolve from and build on one another.

BASIC PROCEDURE ONE

RELAXATION

How it Works

In Part One, we saw that during autonomic arousal it is the *sympathetic* branch of the *autonomic nervous system* (a.n.s.) which triggers off the various physical and mental responses associated with anxiety. We also saw how the *parasympathetic* branch is antagonistic to the activities of the energy-expending *sympathetic* branch and tries to control its excesses. You now know that there is no point in telling yourself to 'calm down' and 'stay cool' because the orders from the *cerebral cortex* go largely unheeded by the *a.n.s.*

Since common sense instructions to 'get a grip on yourself' or to 'unwind' are not going to help, we need another way of controlling the level of arousal in the *sympathetic* branch. The only way in which this can be done is to strengthen the control exerted by the *parasympathetic* branch. Remember the comparison with a see-saw? As one branch goes up, the other must come down. As the level of arousal in the *sympathetic* branch increases, the influence of the *parasympathetic* branch decreases. If we can increase the effect of this latter branch, then *sympathetic* arousal must be brought under control.

To do this, we must carry out some activity which involves a *parasympathetic* response. We know that this branch of the *a.n.s.* is responsible for such activities as digesting food and sexual arousal. This means that if we make our bodies digest food or become sexually aroused, the level of anxiety must come down. It is for this reason that people who are constantly anxious are also often overweight. They eat because, by doing so, they encourage a *parasympathetic* response and so reduce their levels of anxiety. It is also very common for students who have been studying very hard and are under great pressure before an examination to use sexual activity as a means of calming themselves before trying to sleep.

Neither of these methods, however, is really suitable for general anxiety control! If the programme encouraged people to eat whenever they felt anxious, it would be necessary to help them overcome the fresh anxieties produced by feeling obese and unfit! The objections to sexual activity as an everyday means of controlling anxiety are equally practical and even more obvious. There are a number of situations, for example prior to an important examination or interview, when sex can be very helpful. But this is not a procedure which could be generally used in all anxiety based problem situations.

Fortunately, there is a third means of stimulating the *para-sympathetic* branch of the *a.n.s.* This is the procedure of relaxation, which is used in the Anxiety Antidote. Relaxation is an extremely effective means of lowering anxiety by reducing the level of *sympathetic* arousal. It can be learned quite easily and used in every situation where anxiety needs to be brought under control. Since relaxation can never be other than beneficial, you need have no worry that by mastering these procedures you will acquire a fresh set of problems.

Re-Learning Relaxation

As young children, we are able to relax very quickly and deeply, but when we grow older, this skill is lost. We train ourselves to wear a mask in order to conceal our true feelings from the world. This mask involves not only the muscles of the face but of the whole body, as recent research into body language has clearly shown. Muscles are kept unnecessarily tense on so many occasions that after a time we can no longer distinguish between tension and relaxation in the different muscle groups.

Try this simple test. Think about the way you are sitting, lying or standing as you read this book. Which muscles are under tension because they are doing work and which ones are needlessly taut? Concentrate on the muscles of your shoulders, neck, tongue, jaw and forehead. There is probably no good reason why these should be stiff and tense but the chances are that they will be! If you are sitting down, are your hips, lower back and legs relaxed or have you kept them under tension? Notice the way a small child unwinds and flops out when resting. Even if they are lying on the hard surface of an un-carpeted floor, they will probably be completely at ease and cat-like in their relaxation. This is the kind of state we need to achieve. It is not so much a question of learning a new skill as of re-learning something which we could all do with ease during the first few years of life.

When and Where to Carry Out the Training

You will need a quiet room in which it is warm enough to lie motionless for up to twenty minutes without feeling shivery. It should be well ventilated to prevent stuffiness and you may prefer to darken it slightly. It should contain a bed, couch or a comfortable chair. If you are alone at home, take the phone off the hook so that you will not be unexpectedly jerked out of a relaxed state.

If possible, fit in two 15–20 minute practice sessions every day for the first week to ten days of training. It is much better to have regular short sessions than occasional long ones. As you become more skilled, you will not only be able to shorten each training session but carry them out under all kinds of conditions, even at work or while sitting in a car, bus or train.

The exact times of day when you slot in your training will depend on your family commitments and individual preferences. If possible, try carrying out one session when you get home from work and a second just prior to going to sleep. By training at these times, you will derive maximum benefit in the short as well as the long term. As you are mastering the skill, you will find that the short sessions of relaxation practice help you banish fatigue, wind down from the stresses of the day and, when carried out immediately prior to turning off the bedside light, help you enjoy quicker and more restful sleep.

How to Carry Out the Training

There are several ways of learning to relax. Two of the most easily mastered methods will now be described. Begin by trying out the first technique. If you find it too difficult to unwind using this method then switch to the second approach. But give yourself at least two or three days practice before changing training methods. It always takes time to re-learn the once familiar, and natural skill of relaxation – especially if you have been living a very tense and stressful life for a number of years.

Method One

Loosen any tight clothing, take off your shoes and lie down on the bed or couch. If you are relaxing in an easy chair, settle comfortably with your legs stretched out. In both cases, have your arms at your sides with the palms inwards and your legs uncrossed. Unless you find it distressing to do so, close your eyes lightly. If this causes you any anxiety then try to position yourself so that you can look at a fairly neutral background – for example, a plain wall or ceiling. You do not want to have to focus on anything distracting.

Spend a few moments trying to unwind generally. Keep your breathing light and regular. As soon as you start to relax, a whole host of thoughts will probably come chasing into your mind. Merely try to observe them in a detached way, but do not seek to expel them as this will only make you more aroused.

Now, starting with your hands and working your way slowly up towards your shoulders and neck, I want you to think about each part of your body in turn. Focus your attention first of all on your hands and wrists. Note if there is any tension there and if there is ease it away. Concentrate on unwinding

hese muscles and letting them flop out more and more completely. Do the same for the muscles of your arms, shoulders and
neck. Spend about one minute focusing your attention on each
of these muscle groups in turn. Notice any tension and let them
relax. All this time be sure to keep your breathing light and
regular.

Now think about your facial muscles. These are the muscles
of the forehead, eye-lids and eye-brows, lips, jaw, tongue
and throat. Let them all relax as deeply as you can. Have your
eye-lids lightly shut with your eyes looking straight ahead. Or,
f you find this difficult, keep your eyes focused on the most
neutral background you can find. Have your teeth slightly
parted, mouth slightly open.

Now travel down your body. Notice any tension in your
chest. If you have been breathing lightly and regularly, the
muscles of the rib cage and diaphragm should be quite deeply
relaxed. Now think about any tension around your stomach. Do
not try to hold it in. Let the muscles of the abdominal wall flop
out.

Relax your buttocks and thigh muscles. Finally, focus your
attention on the muscles of your calves and ankles. Let these
relax. Devote at least sixty seconds to each of the muscle groups
mentioned above.

In the early stages of training, you may find it difficult to
notice small amounts of tension in these muscles. This is hardly
surprising because your body has grown used to ignoring quite
extensive tension. But, after a little practice, you will find it
increasingly easy to spot tension in the muscle groups and let
them relax.

When you have allowed your body to relax as deeply as
possible, spend five minutes enjoying the sensation of being free
from tension. You may feel slightly chilled at this stage. Do not
worry. It is a good sign which shows that you are relaxing quite
deeply. At all times breathe in and out through your nose,
keeping the breaths light and regular. You may find it helpful
to focus your attention on the word 'Relax'. Each time you

exhale say this word silently to yourself: 'Relax . . . relax . . . relax. . . .' It will help you to stay in a tension-free state.

After a few days, spend the five minutes of tension-free rest in conjuring up some pleasant image in your mind. You may choose a country scene which you remember as being especially tranquil and relaxing; you might prefer to imagine yourself lying on a sun-warmed beach and listening to the surf breaking gently. It does not have to be an outdoor scene. Indeed, you may find that such an image tends to make you anxious. In this case, see yourself indoors, perhaps sitting in a favourite armchair by a warm fire or relaxed and listening to some piece of music which gives you special enjoyment. Some people find it hard to conjure up a vivid image but quite easy to imagine a slowly changing sequence of soothing colours, perhaps accompanied by a gentle and calming piece of music. Whatever your preference, try to make the image as vivid as you can so that it begins to drive out anxiety-provoking thoughts. Do not 'look in' on the scene as though you were a detached observer, but imagine yourself to be a part of that environment. Feel the warmth of the sun or the fire, try to conjure the scent and the sounds of your peaceful and relaxing surroundings.

As with physical relaxation, the ability to form and hold this type of mental imagery will not come all at once. Practise as frequently as possible and build on the image from session to session. Initially, you may only be able to picture the scene for a matter of seconds before distracting thoughts interfere. Do not worry. This is perfectly normal. All these unwanted thoughts will circle while you are attempting, in a relaxed and casual manner, to rebuild the desired surroundings.

At the end of a period of relaxation, get up slowly or you may feel a little light-headed. Go about your normal activities in as calm and relaxed a manner as possible. Carry the good feelings produced by the relaxation training into your normal life.

Method Two

If you find it hard to notice the difference between tension and relaxation, you can overcome the problem by deliberately tensing and then relaxing the muscles. This is a training method described in previous books. It is a very successful procedure, although some people find it slightly more difficult to remember in the early stages.

Start as before by loosening any tight clothing, removing your shoes and settling in a suitable location. Have your feet stretched out and side by side, with your arms at your sides, palms turned inwards.

As in the previous method, the training begins at the hands and works slowly up and then down the body taking in all the major muscle groups. The difference is that, in this case, I am going to show you how to put each of the groups, in turn, under tension.

Tense the muscles of the hands and forearms by clenching your fists as tightly as possible. Squeeze them together as hard as you can and hold the tension for a slow count of five. Now relax them. Let your fingers stretch out and feel the difference between tension and relaxation. Notice how pleasant it feels when the muscles are able to flop out. Rest for a minute, experiencing the pleasant sensation of relaxation in your hands and forearms. During this time, keep your breathing shallow and regular. As you exhale silently repeat the word: 'Relax.'

The next group of muscles to tense are those in the *front* of your upper arms, your biceps. You can tense these by bending your arms at the elbows and trying to touch your wrists to your shoulders. Bend your arms as far as you can and feel the tension this produces. Now hold the position for a slow count to five. Relax. Let your arms drop back with the palms towards your body. Again notice the difference between tension and relaxation in your hands and arms. Spend one minute relaxing as completely as possible and enjoying the sensation of relaxation in the previously very tense muscle groups. Continue to breathe in and out through your nose. Focus on the word 'Relax' each time you exhale and feel yourself sinking more and more deeply into the bed or chair.

The muscles in the back of your upper arms, your triceps, can be tensed by stretching out your arms as hard as you can. Straighten them out. Reach for the ceiling or opposite wall. Feel the tension. Hold the position for a slow count of five. Now relax. Let your arms drop back to your sides. Spend a minute experiencing the sensation of being relaxed and noticing the difference between the muscles which are under tension and those which have been allowed to unwind very deeply. Keep your breathing shallow and regular. Focus on the key word 'Relax' and repeat it silently each time you breathe out.

At this point you may like to carry out a further ten or fifteen minutes more training just by concentrating on different areas of the body in turn, as in Method One, and letting them unwind more and more deeply. You can then go on to memorise further muscle groups during the next session of training. However, if you feel that you can learn more muscle groups in one session (use the summary and memory jogger at the end of this section to help you) then continue as follows with the muscles of the *shoulders*, *neck* and *face*. These muscles are often kept in unnecessary tension even by people who can manage to relax their arm and trunk muscles when they are not in use. We have already mentioned the fact that many adults wear a mask to disguise or conceal their true feelings. Bad posture is another reason why shoulder and neck muscles are needlessly strained. Look around you the next time you walk down a street and notice the number of people who slouch along with their shoulders sagging and necks bent forward. This puts a great deal of unnecessary strain on the muscle groups in the neck, shoulders and back. When sitting down, a combination of bad posture and poor furniture design can add further strain. I am not suggesting that everybody must stride around like marines on parade or sit bolt upright. Indeed, these attitudes can result in just as much needless tension as the slouch. But you should try to move in a relaxed and balanced manner with the weight evenly distributed and your centre of gravity below the base of your spine rather than slightly forward on your feet. By watching out for the way you walk and sit, you could save yourself from unnecessary muscle pains, headaches and fatigue. The ability to move around in a relaxed manner is a skill which you can learn by following the instructions given in Special Procedure One later in this part of the book.

If you are starting a new session of relaxation training at this point, go through the three muscle groups practised earlier before proceeding to the shoulder muscles.

You can tense these by shrugging your shoulders as tightly as you can. Raise your shoulders – higher and higher. Feel the tension which this produces in the shoulder muscles. Hold the shrug for the slow count of five. Now relax. Let your arms drop by your side. Flop out the muscles and notice the difference between tension and relaxation. Experience the pleasant sensations of being deeply relaxed in these muscles. Spend a minute enjoying this pleasant sensation and try to make the muscles unwind still further. Keep your breathing regular and shallow. As you breathe out through your nostrils, repeat the key word: 'Relax . . . relax . . . relax. . . .'

We now come to the muscles on the neck. You can tense these by pressing your head back against the bed, couch or chair as hard as possible. Push down with the back of your head. Push harder and harder. Hold this position for a slow count of five. Now relax. Once again, notice the difference between tension and relaxation. Before going on to the next set of muscles, spend a few moments lying still, breathing lightly and experiencing the feelings of relaxation throughout your body. Focus on the key word 'Relax' while letting your neck and shoulder muscles unwind and become more and more relaxed. Continue the feeling of letting go.

The muscles in your forehead can be tensed by raising your eye-brows as though enquiring. Raise your eye-brows as high as you can. Hold this for a slow count of five. Now relax. Let your eye-brows drop down. Notice the difference between tension and relaxation. Carry on the feeling of letting go while you focus on the key word: 'Relax . . . relax. . . .'

The muscles in your eye-brows and eye-lids can be tensed by frowning as hard as you can. Squeeze your eyes tightly shut. Feel the tension. Hold it for a slow count of five. Now relax. Smooth out your forehead. If you can do so without feeling anxious, keep your eye-lids lightly closed, with your eyes still and gazing straight ahead. Experience the difference between tension and relaxation around your eyes. Keep your breathing shallow and each time you breathe out focus on the key word 'Relax'.

You can tense the muscles in your jaw by biting your teeth together as tightly as you can. Bite them together tightly and feel the tension in your jaw. Hold it for a slow count of five. Now relax. Part your teeth slightly so there is no pressure. Feel the difference between tension and relaxation in your jaw. Enjoy the pleasant sensation of letting go and spend a few moments allowing your jaw to relax more and more deeply while you concentrate on the key word 'Relax'.

The muscles in your tongue and throat can be tensed by putting the tip of your tongue against the roof of your mouth and pushing up as hard as you can. Push up hard – harder. Hold it for a slow count of five. Now relax. Let your tongue drop down to the bottom of your mouth. Keep it still. Feel the difference between tension and relaxation. Feel the tension ease away from your tongue and throat.

The muscles in your lips and face can be tensed by pressing your lips together as tightly as you can. Press your lips together – tighter. Hold it for a slow count of five. Feel the tension in your lips and face. Now relax. Relax your lips and face as deeply as you can. Concentrate on the key word 'Relax' while you continue to let the muscles in your lips and face unwind more and more deeply.

At this point, you might again like to finish the session with some general relaxation, concentrating on the remaining muscle groups in the chest, stomach, hips and legs without actually putting them under tension. If you would prefer to learn all the muscle groups in one session then continue as follows.

Tense the chest muscles by breathing in as deeply as you can. Breathe in and hold it for a slow count to five. Notice the tension in your chest and then relax. Exhale and expel as much air as you can. Let your breathing return to normal, keeping your breaths light and regular. As you breathe out, silently say the key word 'Relax'. Spend a minute noticing the difference between tension and relaxation in all the muscle groups which you have so far worked through.

The stomach muscles can be tensed by flattening the abdominal wall as though preparing to receive a blow. Tighten the muscles as hard as you can and hold this for a slow count of five. Now let the muscles flop out completely. Let your stomach sag. Spend a minute experiencing the difference between tension and relaxation in the major muscle groups.

The muscles in your hips and lower back can be tensed by squeezing your buttocks together very tightly. Squeeze them together and notice the tension this produces. Hold it for a slow count of five. Now relax and spend a minute enjoying this feeling of relaxation and experiencing deep relaxation in most of the major muscle groups. Always bear in mind that your breathing should be shallow and regular. Focus on the key word 'Relax' each time you breathe out.

If you forget one of the muscle groups, or the method of putting a particular set of muscles under tension, then use the table below together with the memory jogger to help you remember.

Muscle Groups	Tensed by
Hands and lower arms	Clenching fists
Front upper arms (biceps)	Bending arms to touch shoulders with wrists
Back upper arms (triceps)	Straightening arms as hard as possible
Chest	Breathing in as deeply as possible
Shoulders	Shrugging hard
Neck	Pushing back head against support
Forehead	Raising eye-brows as though inquiring
Eye-brows and eye-lids	Frowning as hard as you can and squeezing eyes shut
Jaw	Biting teeth together hard
Tongue and throat	Pushing tongue against roof of mouth
Lips and face	Pressing lips together tightly
Stomach	Flattening stomach as though preparing to receive a blow
Hips and lower back	Squeezing buttocks together
Legs	Stretching legs and pointing toes downwards

Memory Jogger for Muscle Groups
You may find it easier to remember these muscle groups if you use the memory jogger: *All New Exercises Must Take Longer.* In this, the first letter of each word stands for one of the major muscle groups which have to be tensed and relaxed:

*A*ll   (Arms and hands)
*N*ew   (Neck and shoulders)
*E*xercises   (Eye-brows, eye-lids and forehead)
*M*ust   (Mouth, lips, tongue and throat)
*T*ake   (Trunk: chest, abdomen and hips)
*L*onger   (Legs)

Sequence
Tense muscles. . . . Hold for a slow count to five. . . . Relax. Unwind and notice the difference between tension and relaxation during the next 60 seconds.

Quick Relaxation

Everybody learns to relax at a different rate. If you are training with your family or partner then be sure to bear this point in mind. Take the training at your own pace. Make every practice session pleasurable by *enjoying* the feelings of relaxation as fully as possible. When you find it easy to relax each of the muscle groups, you need no longer use prior tensing exercises. At this point, too, you can cut out one of the training sessions, if you wish, but start to practise relaxing quickly a number of times each day. Quick relaxation training need only take a couple of minutes per session. Begin by carrying out the quick relaxation procedures detailed below under the most favourable conditions – that is, in the privacy of a quiet room or with your relaxation group under similar conditions. When you become proficient at quick relaxation, start using the skill in real life.

Use it before, during, and after any stressful encounter, in situations where you particularly need to stay relaxed or if you suddenly feel tired. Some especially useful times to carry out short sessions of quick relaxation are:

In the home or office before, during and after a confrontation.
Before and during an interview, examination or test.
In your car before and after a drive through heavy traffic.
In your office or in your car before an important meeting.
Immediately prior to making a speech in public.
At home after a stressful interaction with your partner or children.
On returning home tired after work or shopping.
When going into a room full of strangers, for example at a party or social gathering.
When summoning up the confidence to ask someone for a date.
When anticipating a sexual encounter – if this makes you feel over-anxious.

How You Can Relax Quickly

Sit down in any type of chair. If this is comfortable and gives support for your neck and head, so much the better. But you can still learn quick relaxation in an office chair. Let your hands hang by your sides. Have your legs uncrossed. If you are sitting upright, rest your feet sideways on the floor so that your soles face inwards. Keep your head comfortably balanced and look straight ahead. This position minimises the strain on your shoulder muscles. Your back should be straight.

Now put all the muscle groups under tension at the same time!
Clench your fists.
Bend your arms at the elbows and try to touch wrists to shoulders.

Shrug your shoulders tightly.

Breathe in so that your chest expands as far as possible.

If you have support for the back of the head, press back against it.

Close your eyes tightly.

Frown.

Press the tip of your tongue against the roof of your mouth.

Purse your lips tightly together.

Clench your teeth.

Flatten your stomach.

Squeeze your buttocks together.

Straighten your legs.

Hold this position for a slow count of five. Now relax, let go completely and allow all your muscles to flop out as quickly as possible. As you do so, notice the difference between tension and relaxation. Keep your breathing shallow and regular. Focus on the key word 'Relax' each time you breathe out through your nose. Let your eyes remain still and looking ahead. Keep your teeth apart, lips slightly open. Smooth out your forehead. Let your tongue drop back into your mouth. Keep your arms by your side. Let your shoulders and stomach sag.

After training in this way for a little while, you should find that you can relax without any prior tensing. Merely by settling back and silently repeating 'Relax' as you breathe in and out, lightly and regularly, you will find that you relax automatically. When this happens you will know that you have recaptured the childhood skill of being able to flop out and unwind at will.

You should start to relax without having to think about it as your body notices unnecessary tension and responds with the relaxation response.

Practise relaxation in this way as often as you can, so as to keep the skill fresh. They need not be lengthy training sessions. As little as thirty seconds quick relaxation carried out at any convenient moment will maintain the skill at a high level. If you enjoy the feeling of deep muscle relaxation, with or without prior tension exercises, then continue with several sessions each week just for the pleasure and benefit it brings.

Relax when travelling to and from work, while riding up and down in a lift, when you are waiting to see somebody, during your morning and afternoon breaks. This easily acquired skill can make a great difference to your whole life. Not only will you find it much easier to manage anxiety-generating situations but you should tire much less easily and you will probably suffer far fewer aches and pains, including cramps, back trouble and headaches, as needless tension is banished from your life.

Differential Relaxation

The final relaxation skill I want you to learn is differential relaxation. This will come very easily and naturally, once you have mastered deep muscle relaxation.

The idea behind differential relaxation is simple. With practice, you can learn to keep the muscle groups which are not required to be under tension, loose and relaxed. This allows you to remain free from unnecessary strain even when engaged in some physically vigorous activity. It can also be used to advantage in many less strenuous pursuits, where a relaxed confidence enhances performance.

How to Learn Differential Relaxation

After a period of either quick or deep relaxation, sit up slowly but do not try to stand. Simply open your eyes and look around the room. Remain perfectly still in every other part of your body. Only make your eye-balls move as you study your surroundings. Observe as many details as possible of the area in which you are relaxing. While doing so, notice what it feels like to be moving your eyes around while every other part of your body remains relaxed and free from tension. After 30 seconds or so, start to turn your head so that you can take in even more of your surroundings. Keep your head movements slow and relaxed. Tilt your head from side to side. Notice what it feels like to have the muscles of the neck and eyes under tension while the rest of the body remains quite relaxed.

Now say something. It does not matter what. Talk to yourself for a few seconds. Experience the feeling of moving your lips and tongue while the rest of the body is relaxed.

When you have done this, move your fingers as though you were playing the piano. Now move your arms and fingers. Keep all the movements very slow. As before, I want you to notice what it feels like to have some of the muscle groups working while the remainder are relaxed and at ease.

Stand up and start to move slowly around the room. Let your arms hang by your sides with the fingers motionless. Walk around for a few moments to get used to the sensation of moving about in a relaxed and easy manner. Now return to the chair and sit down. Try to relax all over again simply by letting your body flop. Keep your breathing regular and light. Let the tension slip away from your muscles. Now stand up and return to your normal activities.

Differential relaxation is not a difficult skill to master, provided that you have become reasonably skilled in the two other forms of relaxation. Practise for several days but, as soon as you feel confident enough to do so, start to use differential relaxation in real life situations. When you are out walking, for instance, notice if there is any unnecessary tension in your face, shoulders or arm muscles. If there is *relax* those muscles. Ease away the needless strain. If you are travelling in a car, bus or train, watch out for tension in muscles which are not being called on to do any hard work. Are your shoulders relaxed? Are you frowning or screwing up your eyes? Is your mouth tightly shut? Are your hands clenched into fists? Let these muscles unwind. Unwind and ease away the strain, which is only causing you to feel stressed and needlessly fatigued. Let your shoulders drop. Smooth out your brow. Slightly open your jaws and let your tongue drop to the bottom of your mouth. Relax your fingers.

Train yourself to notice any unnecessary tension, especially when you feel under stress. If you are playing a competitive sport, then only use those muscle groups essential to the game. The rest of your body should remain completely relaxed.

---

*Summary of Training**

Differential Relaxation is the skill of being able to relax muscle groups which are not being actively used.

Practise by using different muscle groups in turn while keeping the rest of your body very relaxed.

Start with the eyes, then the neck muscles.

Talk while remaining still and at ease.

Move your fingers and then your arms.

Stand up and move around in a very relaxed way.

Teaching Relaxation to Children

As already stressed, young children are the real experts at relaxation and, in many cases, find it far easier than their parents who will have spent years forgetting the skill and replacing their natural ability to unwind with anxiety and tension responses.

However, since, in certain circumstances, children may find it difficult or too tedious to follow the full adult programme, we have modified the training schedule and included some guidelines to follow when teaching this skill to children.

Start by reading through the instructions in the adult programme and, preferably, commence your own course of training. Learn the major muscle groups and the ways in which they can be tensed. Once you are confident in your knowledge of the techniques, proceed as follows:

* If you have any difficulty learning these techniques, it may help to send for details of a relaxation training cassette, available from LIFESKILLS, 3 Brighton Road, London N2 8JU.

(1) Find a place where the child or children can relax. This is much more flexible than for adults since the emphasis on a quiet room is not so great, although major distractions, such as television or other children who are not taking part in the training, should be avoided. The child can lie on a bed, couch or floor. If the weather is fine, there is no reason why the exercises should not be practised out of doors. A grassy field, a garden or a fairly deserted sandy beach are excellent places in which to combine training and sun-bathing. It is important to make the sessions as enjoyable as possible in order to keep the child interested and motivated.

(2) Fix a regular time to practise so that the child is always expecting the training session. Good times are either on arrival home from school or just before going to bed, when they will help the child to wind down from the stresses of the day and prepare for a relaxed sleep. This can be of special benefit to children with nightmare or bed-wetting problems. (See also Family and Children section in Part Three.)

(3) In addition to the set periods of relaxation training, we recommend that you make use of play activities to introduce additional relaxation practice. For example, the body is in a particularly receptive state for training following a period of physical exertion. The natural end to a game of rough and tumble or a sport which involved a lot of vigorous activity is a few minutes of relaxation.

(4) In order to sustain motivation, it will be useful to introduce a reward system. As I explained in Part One, the use of such positive reinforcers helps to establish new pieces of behaviour and speeds up the learning process. You could use a token system whereby the child receives a plastic token or similar object which has been given some kind of face value. For example, six tokens might 'buy' a book or magazine, two tokens some sweets or fruit. Reward the child with these tokens after each

session of relaxation. But this should be done in *addition* to any treats which are normally made available, not as a substitute for them. Unless you do this, the relaxation training and the tokens may be seen as a form of punishment. Remember too, that for maximum effect, reinforcers must be introduced immediately following the piece of behaviour.

(5) Find out your child's favourite TV show, game or story book hero. During relaxation training, encourage the child to imagine or fantasise about these enjoyable subjects. This will tend to increase the level of para-sympathetic arousal and so enhance the relaxation response.

(6) Once it has been explained to them, most children find it very easy to master the skill and there should be no need to take the training a little at a time. Indeed, if you spread it too thinly, interest and motivation may decline. The best method is to begin with the quick relaxation procedure described earlier in which all the muscle groups are tensed and then relaxed at once.

Tell the child to lie flat on his or her back. Then:

(i) Clench the fists to tense the hands and lower arms.

(ii) Bend the arms at the elbows, trying to touch the wrists to the shoulders to tense the biceps.

(iii) Shrug the shoulders up into the neck to tense the shoulders and upper back.

(iv) Press the head back into the floor or bed to tense the neck.

(v) Squeeze the eyes tightly shut to tense the forehead and eye-lids.

(vi) Bite the teeth together, press the tongue against the roof of the mouth and press the lips together to tense the mouth area.

(vii) Tighten the stomach muscles as though preparing to receive a blow.

(viii) Stretch out the legs and squeeze the buttocks together to tense the muscles of the hips, lower back and legs.

(ix) Finally, take a deep breath to tense the muscles of the chest.

All this should be accomplished within about ten seconds and the position held for another seven or eight seconds. Then let all the muscles relax deeply and quickly and exhale. The process of 'letting go' should be described. Ask the child or children to notice the difference between tension and relaxation in their various muscle groups.

As we saw earlier, it is helpful if, while encouraging the child to continue relaxing until the limbs become heavy, you encourage fantasies about the favourite TV show, game or hero so as to increase the pleasurable feelings associated with relaxation.

(7) Continue with one or more sessions of relaxation training daily for about a week. By the end of this time, the child should have developed the ability to relax deeply and quickly. If it takes longer, however, do not worry. As we saw earlier everybody learns relaxation at their own speed and it is very important not to force the pace.

With older children, there is sometimes a reluctance to carry out relaxation training because they: 'Don't see the point.' You should be able to arouse their interest in the procedure if you point out that it will help them in some area of special importance to them. For example, you could explain that the ability to relax will help them play a favourite sport better, make them more confident in social situations, give them a greater chance of success in examinations and reduce the anxieties which are often felt during the early stages of learning to date members of the opposite sex.

BREATHING

One of the most common correlates of anxiety and exhaustion is hyperventilation. This simply means over-breathing and is demonstrated in several different forms between people. It may be seen as frequent sighing; snatched breathing at the beginning of sentences and during rapid or pressurised speech; stertorous breathing or holding in of the breath; or a tendency to pant.

Any form of hyperventilation will typically be carried out as upper chest respiration – the use of the chest cavity itself to expand and contract in order to pull air in and out. This is exactly the wrong way to breathe under normal circum-stances, since air should be sucked in and expelled by the action of the diaphragm at the bottom of the rib-cage which should behave like a set of bellows. The rib-cage itself should remain relatively still and the diaphragm should be observed in operation as a rising and falling of the stomach or solar plexus areas.

The main problem associated with upper chest respiration is that an incorrect quantity of oxygenated air is usually brought into the lungs. Usually, the quantity is higher than needed. This results in a greater transmission of oxygen into the bloodstream than is required and, since the haemoglobin in the blood selectively prefers oxygen to carbon dioxide, some of the necessary carbon dioxide in the bloodstream is displaced by an excess of oxygen. We do not normally think of oxygen as being poisonous, though an excess of it, as with many other normally beneficial chemicals, can produce toxic effects.

At an acute level, one of these effects is the sensation, paradoxically, of suffocation. Thus, when the bloodstream becomes too rich in oxygen, the victim experiences a sense of suffocation and begins to gulp in even more oxygen-rich air. The vicious circle proceeds and a hyperventilation panic attack or anxiety surge can ensue. In fact, recent research has indicated that as many as 80 per cent of the population complaining of anxiety attacks can be helped to eradicate these simply by training in normal breathing techniques.

A more lasting effect of hyperventilation is chronic tension around the chest and shoulders area, producing chest pains which are often the source of anxiety for victims who begin to believe they may be cardiac risks. Further complaints can include tingling in the limbs; dizziness and derealisation; sweating and palpitations; and even waking in the night and early in the morning with panic attacks as the hyperventilation continues during sleep.

The most crucial stage in controlling hyperventilation and producing normal breathing is monitoring. Many sufferers, after being told only a few times during the course of an hour's consultation, can spot when they are about to hyperventilate or have just done so. This awareness is quite rapid to build up and is simply a case of noticing any of the tell-tale signs of hyperventilation mentioned above and asking one or two members of the family to point it out to them when it occurs.

The next stage in normal breathing training is to spend a few minutes every hour during the day sitting or standing with one hand placed on the epigastrium (the stomach area) and one hand on the upper rib-cage. Breathing should then be carried out so that the hand on the upper chest area remains quite still and that on the epigastrium moves up and down noticeably. This may feel extremely strange to someone who chronically hyperventilates, though it quite quickly becomes much more comfortable with repeated practice.

The third stage of training is to prevent the spiralling effect of hyperventilation once it has started, perhaps in a situation of stress or threat. Here, the best technique of all is simply to stop breathing for a time. This should be done by pausing after a long exhalation, and certainly not by holding the breath in. The technique of holding the breath out should be practised frequently in safe or secure situations so that it is a well-developed skill at those times when it is needed as a stress management intervention. The variants on this technique, such as breathing in and out of a paper bag and breathing in and out of cupped hands over the mouth and nose, are quite valid, as all the techniques are intended to reduce the oxygen level in the blood stream and increase the carbon dioxide level. However, breathing out and holding the breath out has the advantage of being non-observable and can therefore be used even in such complex and public situations as TV interview appearances, public speaking and job interviews.

BASIC PROCEDURE TWO

SLEEP PROTECTION

There are several factors which are relevant to good sleeping habits and these can all be divided into a series of 'dos' and 'don'ts'. Overridingly, however, it is important to remember that both quantity and quality of sleep are important in combating the effects of strain and the exhaustion. If you consider that you are going through a particularly stressed or troubled period and that your sleep in general has become less beneficial, you should make every effort to cut back on social engagements and work functions which are likely to erode your sleeping habits. It is a good idea anyway to give over about one weekend in every two months to a regime of early nights and afternoon sleeps – preferably with the whole family participating. With that proviso, the following list of strategies, regularly carried out, should facilitate better sleeping:

(1) *Exercise*. It is perfectly true that insomnia is the curse of the sedentary occupations and that tired muscles which have been healthily worked during the day build up a chemical waste which has soporific effects and enables sleep to come more easily. If you do not take much exercise and are not inclined to, try just taking five minutes in the evening using the Canadian Air Force exercises for men and women. These provide a vigorous workout with a minimum of time investment yet can produce the chemistry associated with muscle tissue break-down.

(2) *Sex*. As a pleasurable variant on exercise, together with its usually associated sensations of support, comfort and well-being with a loved one, sex can help the sleep

process considerably. The post-sex resolution or 'afterglow' state is one which is neurophysiologically consistent with the sleep state. It is also worth commenting that a good sex life is one of the early things to be disrupted during states of stress, and so encouraging the maintenance of a healthy sex life can be beneficial at many levels.

(3) *Napping*. Napping in the early evening can have disastrous effects on ability to fall asleep later. The most important component of sleep, rapid eye movement or REM sleep, during which we dream, is most plentiful just after we have fallen asleep and then occurs in shorter and shorter bursts during the night. Most people will experience only about two hours of REM sleep, the first half-hour of which typically occurs on falling asleep. So, if you have napped during the early part of the evening, you will have had possibly 25 per cent of your nightly REM sleep need and may well dull your appetite for REM sleep when you go to bed. For this reason, try to avoid actually falling asleep during the evening before retiring to bed for the night.

(4) *Relaxation*. Whilst you should try to avoid napping during the evening, it is extremely beneficial to carry out fifteen to twenty minutes of relaxation exercises in order to emphasise the ending of the work part of the day and the beginning of the leisure and recuperation part. Such exercises are probably best carried out during the early part of the evening, to separate the more active part of the day from the more personal and relaxed. They can, however, be used on actually retiring to bed as the state induced by relaxation is also very conducive to sleeping.

(5) *Diet*. What you take in by way of food and drink may also affect your sleep patterns. It is fairly well known that many people respond with sleep difficulties to cheese and dairy products. However, remember that

chilli peppers can affect your metabolism some hours after eating them and can have you waking in the night with palpitations! More commonly, remember that whilst alcohol can relax you and put you into a pleasant and sleepy condition, it can also wake you in the middle of the night with similar palpitations and sweating. This is because alcohol contains congeners which, upon being metabolised by the body, break down into compounds which can make you 'speed up'. The technique is to find which alcohol – always taken in moderation – affects you least. One hint to go by is that the more aged and vintage alcohols tend to be the most toxic or rich in congeners whilst good white wine and vodka tend to be the purest.

(6) *Ruminations*. Most of us have experienced the problem of going to bed at night, fully intending to sleep, and then finding that our thoughts are tumbling over one another in a state of confusion and gradually mounting urgency. We remember things to do the next day and worry about the things in the day just gone. As we toss and turn and build up an increasing state of tension, the likelihood of falling asleep rapidly diminishes. At 4 a.m. we may fall into a sleep based on exhaustion and wake in the morning feeling worse than we did the day before. One of the best ways of dealing with intrusive thoughts or ruminations is to externalise them, and for most people the best way of doing this is by writing them on a sheet of paper. Certainly, if you have gone to bed and find yourself ruminating, then waste no time in getting up and spilling out all the thoughts onto paper. If you feel that you may ruminate when you go to bed, then try to do your outpourings before you retire.

(7) *The Sleep Paradox*. Remember that the more you try to will or force yourself to fall asleep, the harder sleep will be to achieve. By contrast, the less bothered you are about falling asleep, the more likely you are to do so.

So if you feel it may be difficult to fall asleep when you go to bed, decide as you put your head on the pillow that you will give yourself fifteen minutes to get to sleep and then get up again for fifteen minutes of light reading, shoe cleaning, briefcase packing or any other activity which does not involve deep thought. If you have to get up and go back to bed again after fifteen minutes, make the same deal with yourself for a second time. Even if you have to get up two or three times in this way, you will eventually fall asleep and do so after only a few minutes of going to bed. Learning to fall asleep through exhaustion is extremely erosive, and this technique helps to prevent that. Most commonly, however, people fall asleep in the first or second fifteen-minute period as, paradoxically, when you have decided that you do not care whether you go to sleep or not because you have an alternative strategy, sleep often comes with ease.

BASIC PROCEDURE THREE

POSITIVE SELF-TALK

How it Works

In Part One, I described how the panic spiral develops out of a mixture of distressing bodily responses and negative mental statements about the inevitability of failure. You have now learnt a skill, Relaxation Training, which will shortly be used to control the bodily responses. But it is equally important to be able to banish the negative statements and replace them with Positive Self-Talk, which comprises strategies for coping productively with the problem anxiety situation.

To be successful, the Positive Self-Talk statements must:

(1) Be closely relevant to the situation which causes anxiety at that moment of time.
(2) Be realistic, so that the difficulties are acknowledged rather than ignored and a practical solution is offered.

For example, let us look at what can happen to a person who becomes extremely anxious while trying to stand up for his or her rights in the face of aggressive criticism. Lacking knowledge of the Anxiety Antidote, such a person will probably either apologise and attempt to placate the aggressor or remain completely tongue tied. During this time, they may be experiencing several physical responses, a churning stomach and rapidly beating heart, for instance, and thinking very negatively: 'I've got to get away. I can't cope. I am being made to look such a fool. I can never handle this sort of situation.' The result of the anxiety response is an inability to defend themselves or express their viewpoint, followed by as swift an escape from the situation as possible. As I explained in Part One, such an escape tactic, by relieving the painful anxiety symptoms, is being *negatively reinforced*. This means that it is far more likely to be repeated in any subsequent confrontation. Furthermore, the feelings of humiliation which result are likely to make the individual depressed, lacking in confidence and more liable to experience negative thoughts in similar situations: 'I've failed before. I will fail this time . . .' is a typical and usually self-fulfilling prophesy.

A person who is familiar with Positive Self-Talk strategies should be able to cope with the aggression effectively and counter the attack by thinking and acting on such positive statements as:

'It may be difficult but I am going to stress my major argument for the fourth time because they clearly have taken no notice of the last three and I am going to do it now.'

'This person is clearly too enraged at present to listen to my point-of-view so I will ask them to discuss it with me later and then turn and leave the room without hesitation.'

'Although they are so biased that they may not fully appreciate my point-of-view, I will continue to refuse to do even more overtime although it is being suggested that I am not pulling my weight.'

While such positive mental statements seem no more than common sense, they are extremely difficult for the severe anxiety sufferer to bring to mind. In fact, in order for them to build up such positive and practical self-talk, it is necessary to construct this kind of statement gradually over a number of actual or imagined encounters with the anxiety situation. For most people, it will be easier to use imagined situations at first, to develop the basic essentials of the Positive Self-Talk, and then to increase their strength and realism by using them in practice.

How to Carry Out the Training

In order to begin the Positive Self-Talk training, it is necessary for you to construct a short graded list of anxiety situations. If you have more than one major area of anxiety, you should construct a list or hierarchy for each and deal with them in a similar way. In constructing your rough working hierarchy, it is important to have a detailed description of various representative situations in terms of the time and place when they occur; people present; objects, animate and inanimate, present; mood and general thoughts usually present in the situation; and any other relevant details which make the description true to life. You will probably find that you can quite quickly and easily construct a working hierarchy for your major anxieties from memory. For example, a person who is anxious about travelling may have a graded list which reads as follows:

(1) Travel over short distances while
    driving a car.
(2) Travel by bus.
(3) Travel in an almost empty train.   Increased
(4) Travel as passenger in car over long   Anxiety Felt.
    distances.
(5) Travel in crowded bus or train.
    And so on. . . .

An executive with anxiety problems might devise a list as follows:

(1) Handling excessive work load.
(2) Boardroom negotiations.   Increased
(3) Disciplining a subordinate.   Anxiety Felt.
(4) Dealing with an aggressive client.
(5) Heated exchanges with a superior.
    And so on. . . .

A wife made anxious by her husband might construct the following hierarchy:

(1) Discussions about holiday plans.
(2) Discussions over family budget.
(3) Asking for something extra for the
    house.
(4) Talking about our marriage
    difficulties.
(5) Defending the children from his
    criticisms.
        And so on. . . .

Increased
Anxiety Felt.

If you are unable to construct such a list from memory, it will
be necessary to keep records over the next few days in order to
build up a collection of anxiety-producing situations. Note
down as many details as possible; where, when and why the
anxiety arose, who was present and what they said or did, how
you felt mentally and physically. These notes need not be a
blow-by-blow account of the situation but they should be
complete enough for you to recall the circumstances clearly
when you read through them.

You will find it most helpful if you collect the information
under three headings:

(1) What happened.
(2) What I thought.
(3) How I felt.

Make up notes any time you feel anxious. This could be when
anticipating a stressful encounter, immediately after such a
confrontation or sometime later if you were still experiencing
anxiety difficulties as a result of that situation.

Example One—Typical entries in records of housewife

WHAT HAPPENED	WHAT I THOUGHT	HOW I FELT
At home. 6.00 p.m. Waiting for husband to come home. Children with me. Worried about telling him that big bill has arrived for telephone. Remembering rows we have had in past over money.	Confused about best way of breaking news. Cannot settle or concentrate on work.	Feel sick. Stomach uncomfortable. Sweating. Mouth dry. Hands shaking.
Argument over bill. Children present. 6.30 p.m. In kitchen. Room hot and stuffy. Husband furious and shouts. Hits table with fists.	Cannot remember what I wanted to say. Very confused. Thoughts racing across mind. Think I will faint.	Body shaking. Heart racing. Feel very sick. Mouth dry. Sweating.
7.30 p.m. At dinner. Alone with husband. He still angry. Says little.	Feel lightheaded. Cannot concentrate. Keep remembering row.	Too sick to eat much. Mouth dry. Hands tremble. Headache.

Example Two—Typical entries in records of businessman

WHAT HAPPENED	WHAT I THOUGHT	HOW I FELT
Driving to office through rush hour traffic. 8.45 a.m. Sunny day. Alone in car. Thinking. Anticipating criticism from other directors over level of business.	Confused. Uncertain what to do. Find it hard to concentrate on driving.	Feel slightly sick. Mouth very dry. Heart beating faster than usual.
11.30 a.m. In Meeting. Boardroom. Three managers and five directors present. Presenting reasons for reduction in level of sales.	Unable to marshall my thoughts or present favourable arguments effectively. Forget details and constantly refer to notes. Concentration poor.	Hands tremble. Feel very sick. Mouth dry. Heart racing. Sweating heavily.
1.00 p.m. At lunch in restaurant with client. Crowded and hot.	Keep on remembering bad Meeting. Cannot pay attention to what client is saying. Cannot recall important facts about his policies.	Still feel rather sick. Stomach cramped. Damp with sweat. Hands unsteady.

Now choose one of the anxiety situations which are low on your graded list and, while lying in a relaxed state, imagine it as vividly as you can. If you have been keeping records, use the details which were noted down to help you build up the scene as accurately as possible.

Notice whether imagining the situation makes you feel in any way anxious. If it does, then you will be able to remember this fact during Anxiety Management Training. For the moment, however, just watch out for any negative thoughts which may come to mind when you are thinking about the situation. When you have gone through it in your mind's eyes, write down all of these statements. Watch out especially for comments like: 'I cannot cope . . . everything is going wrong . . . I am feeling faint . . . I am losing control.'

Adopt a similar procedure with each of the situations on your list, working through the hierarchy from the least worrying to the most anxiety-producing. At the end of this procedure, you should have built up a list of Negative Self-Talk statements.

The third step is to construct Positive Self-Talk statements based on these negative comments. For example, instead of the internal statement: 'I cannot cope', try to look at the situation in more detail and think of some ways in which you could make it more bearable or more to your advantage. You can then begin to construct statements in the form of instructions: 'It will be difficult but I think I can manage it if I. . . .' or 'I shall feel like trying to get out of the situation but I shall stay there as comfortably as possible by relaxing and. . . .' In other words, find something positive about the situation – a sound, colour, person, posture or any other feature or action – which you can focus on to lower the stress level. Returning to the earlier lists, the anxiety sufferers involved might develop Positive Self-Talk along these lines:

Travel Difficulties

SELF-TALK STATEMENTS

'This train journey will be a severe test for me but I know that looking out of the window to watch the passing countryside helps to make it more pleasant so I will concentrate on doing that whenever I feel myself becoming anxious.' Or: 'This car journey is bound to make me feel slightly anxious but I coped well last time by listening to soothing music and reclining the seat so that I could relax more easily.'

Executive Anxiety

SELF-TALK STATEMENTS

'There will be a lot of pressure brought to bear by my boss but I know that if I just say "no" to extra work and avoid being made to feel guilty, my work load will not become even more crippling than it already is.' Or: 'I always hate having to discipline a subordinate but I know that if I walk around the office while doing so I become less anxious than if I remain trapped by my desk and chair.'

Marital Anxiety

SELF-TALK STATEMENTS

'I know that my husband will be angry about the need to spend more money on the children's clothes but he will not be able to make me feel guilty if I remember how much he spends on cigarettes each week.' Or: 'I know that it will be hard to persuade him to talk about our personal problems but I will not become so easily discouraged if I remember how important the marriage is to me.'

Notice how these statements relate directly to a specific piece of behaviour which the person is going to attempt and that they do not make unrealistic claims for the outcome. They do not say, for example: 'I am going to succeed whatever happens . . .' 'I am not going to let myself be bullied . . .' 'I am certainly going to get my own way for once.' This is the way many people, untrained in the techniques of Positive Self-Talk, phrase their inner statements. The danger is that anything less than total achievement will be regarded as failure. If the person does not achieve everything they set out to achieve, is bullied after putting up a good initial assertion response, or does not get entirely their own way, they may well feel disillusioned. Instead of thinking: 'Well the outcome wasn't exactly as I hoped, but I did manage to get this point over' or 'I was pushed around to some extent but he didn't get things all his own way . . .' they chalk up another personal disaster. In any future encounters, their negative self-talk repertoire may well include statements such as: 'I tried to act assertively last time and that was useless' or 'When I attempted before to resist his bullying I came off as badly as ever. Why bother?'

By making it clear to yourself at the outset that there will be difficulties and that you *may not* achieve everything you want out of the situation, you are establishing realistic goals.

After a session in which you used Positive Self-Talk statements, debrief. Think back over the encounter and remember what you said to yourself before and during the confrontation. If you discovered some approach or strategy which helped you through then incorporate this into your next set of Positive Self-Talk statements. Build on any success, however small it may appear in relation to your overall problem. After an encounter, congratulate yourself on achieving any improvements over past behaviour in similar situations. Do not compare yourself with somebody who can apparently deal with the situation effortlessly. Instead, notice how you came a step closer to being able to cope and feel pleased with yourself for having done so.

In Part Three, you will find a large number of strategies which can be incorporated into Positive Self-Talk statements. Start reading the appropriate section of this part of the book now and begin to use the strategies to help you through current anxiety difficulties.

BASIC PROCEDURE FOUR

ANXIETY MANAGEMENT

How it Works

In Part One, we saw how an anxiety spiral can rapidly develop from the initial startle response as a result of negative feedback between mind and body. One method of preventing this spiral from arising is to notice the sensation of the startle, which is usually experienced as an uncomfortable jolt in the stomach, immediately it occurs and then to relax consciously. This will effectively control the anxiety but there is always the danger that you will miss the first warning of anxiety. If you are very busy or preoccupied, the initial startle sensation may occur almost without your realising it. By the time you collect yourself and start thinking about relaxation, the anxiety spiral will have started. While it is very easy to control a low level of anxiety, such as is present immediately following the feeling of 'startle', it becomes increasingly difficult to exert any effective control once the spiral has started to develop. If at this stage you try to relax, there may be such a high level of *sympathetic* arousal that it takes time to counter it with *parasympathetic* arousal. Relaxation will prove effective if you persist with it but many people become additionally anxious when relaxation does not have the immediate effect of calming them down. Believing that their main weapon in the fight has proved useless, they hoist the white flag and resign themselves to another victory for their anxiety response. This makes it all the harder for them to cope successfully with stressful situations in the future. Now their Negative Self-Talk includes such fatalistic statements as: 'I wasn't able to cope last time, not even using relaxation. Obviously the Antidote doesn't work for me. I must be a really bad case of nerves!'

A much safer and more reliable method of Anxiety Management is to train your body to the startle response instantly and
automatically with relaxation. Once this has been achieved, you
need no longer constantly be on the alert for the initial surge of
fear. Even if you fail to notice it, your body will do so and
respond with the correct counter-measure.

The difference between watching out for 'startle' and then
deliberately relaxing and having the kind of automatic response
provided by this form of Anxiety Management, can be illustrated by imagining the fire precautions in use at two different
factories. One has old fashioned equipment. When flames are
spotted somebody presses the alarm bell and men hurry to the
scene with extinguishers which they play on the blaze. Provided
the fire is noticed early enough, everything may be all right. But
there must always be a serious risk that the flames will take hold
before the alarm can be sounded. The other factory has an
automatic sprinkler system connected to heat sensitive devices
placed at strategic points around the building. As soon as a fire
starts, the area is automatically sprayed with water and the
flames quenched. Because a blaze is never allowed to develop,
fire fighting is quick and sure.

Anxiety Management gives you this sort of instant response
to all types of fears. But more than that, it allows you to control
the level of anxiety which you *want* to experience. You can
automatically quench it after the startle response or, if you want
to do so, you can over-ride the relaxation and let the anxiety
build to a desired level before bringing it under control. This
is very valuable because, as we saw in Part One, there are
many situations where it is very helpful to have the body more
than usually keyed up. A moderate degree of arousal improves
performance in a wide range of physical and intellectual
activities. You become more alert and better at co-ordinating
muscular responses. Your reflexes are faster and your visual and
auditory perceptions keener. You are stronger, quicker and
more agile. Such arousal is normally present when playing a
competitive sport, at times of physical danger or if you are

carrying out a skilled and potentially risky activity such as flying an aircraft or driving at speed. It also frequently occurs when you go to a party where a large number of strangers are present, while attending an interview or sitting for an examination, speaking in public or making love in private. Provided the level can be monitored and controlled, this arousal is beneficial. But if it spirals into an anxiety attack, it will obviously be impossible to perform well in any of the activities I have described. Alcohol and tranquillising drugs, the most commonly used anxiety preventers, offer an all-or-nothing solution because they work by chemically depressing the central nervous system. As a result, fears are calmed, anxiety symptoms vanish and a feeling of relaxation may be created. But the price paid is usually a heavy one. The mind works more slowly, the memory is less efficient, physical responses are inhibited, ability and co-ordination are impaired. In the past, drugs may have been the only answer to your anxiety problems. But now you will discover that Anxiety Management offers the same degree of relief from distressing symptoms with the enormous bonus of almost total control.

How to Learn Anxiety Management

Training sessions are most conveniently carried out with the help of a sympathetic friend or relative. If it is impossible for you to find anybody to help, then read the special note at the end of these training instructions and use one of the suggested procedures.

The sequence of events during training sessions is simple.

Relax ⟶ Startle Response ⟶ Control using Relaxation

You put it into effect as follows. Begin by going through quick relaxation so that you feel completely free from tension. Now ask your helper to startle you by making a loud noise at any time during the following ten seconds. It is important that you should know that the sound *is* going to occur but not that you know exactly *when*.

The sound can be produced by smacking a rolled newspaper onto a table top, by slapping the table with the flat of the hand or simply by sharply clapping the hands together.

When the noise occurs, even though you have been expecting it, you will experience the sensation of startle indicating that a spurt of adrenalin has been released into your bloodstream. Respond by immediately making yourself relax all over again. Let your muscles unwind and see how quickly and easily it is possible to bring the initial sensation of anxiety under your complete control. When you are relaxed again, ask your helper to repeat the noise. Once again, a sharp hand clap or the crack of a newspaper striking a flat surface should be sufficient to give you that small spurt of initial anxiety. You do not want to become over-aroused during this training. What you want to achieve is the lowest level of anxiety arousal which you can notice and use as a signal for relaxation. You will achieve this quite satisfactorily if the sound is moderately loud and comes without prior warning.

As before, use the startle response as a signal that you must relax. Unwind again. Keep your breathing shallow and regular. Focus on the key word 'Relax' each time you breathe out.

Carry out one more sequence of startle and relaxation during this training period. You may find that on the third occasion the noise produces much less startle than on the previous occasions. This is because you are getting used to it. In the language of psychology, you are *habituating* to the stimulus.

If you can fit in two periods of Anxiety Management training each day so much the better, but leave a gap of several hours between each session so that you continue to experience the startle response.

Note for People without Helpers

If you are unable to get anybody to help you in your training then you must find some way of producing the startle response noise for yourself. A special training cassette containing instructions and a series of appropriate noises has been recorded by the present author and is available through Lifeskills. There is no reason why you should not make up your own training tape by recording suitably loud noises on a portable tape machine. Allow a reasonable period between each set of noises so that you can relax and unwind after the startle response. About two minutes between each sound should be sufficient.

If you do not have a tape recorder, then you will have to find some mechanical means for generating sound. One way, which has been used successfully by a number of people, is to balance a tin tray between the backs of two upright chairs. Place some knives and forks on the tray to add to the amount of noise. Tie a length of string to one of the chairs and, when you want to produce the startle response, jerk the string and cause the tray to drop. This procedure works very well but it does mean that you have to get up after each 'crash' to reconstruct your 'noise maker'. Before you do so, make certain that you have fully relaxed. When you get up to re-set the tray move slowly and stay as relaxed as you can.

Anxiety Management with Imaginary Situations

After a few days practice, you will find that your body has learned to use the startle response as a signal for it to relax. You can now move on to the final stage in anxiety management training which involves the use of the list/s of anxiety-producing situations which you used during Positive Self-Talk training. Start with the lowest item on your hierarchy and, while sitting comfortably and relaxing, imagine it as vividly as you can. When you notice any anxiety beginning to occur, you should now carry out your quick relaxation as you did in response to the startle which you experienced with loud noises and, at the same time, introduce the positive self-talk statements into the situation and imagine yourself performing confidently in the way that your positive self-talk suggests. Practise this situation several times until you are confident about switching on the relaxation response and the positive self-talk response immediately you feel any anxiety occur. Then you should move on to the next situation and do the same until finally you have worked through the hierarchy. Besides practising positive self-talk in your imagination, you should also picture yourself carrying out the activity in an unhurried and relaxed way. The more slowly and calmly you go through the image, the more ideas and strategies you are likely to develop for dealing with the situation.

Anxiety Management in Real Life Situations

When you are able to handle anxiety in imaginary situations you can start putting the Antidote to work for you in real life. You should find little difficulty in doing this provided you follow a few basic rules.

In the early stages of training, spend a few minutes relaxing before you attempt any of the situations. Only work on one of the anxiety situations at a time and try to start with the lowest and least difficult on your hierarchy list. Go through the scene once again in your imagination and rehearse the Positive Self-Talk statements you may shortly be using. When you have done this, stand up and move around using Differential Relaxation to keep you at ease.

Now rehearse the situation again, this time imagining that your surroundings are those in which the anxiety producing encounter will take place. Use props and, if you have sympathetic friends or relatives, people to assist you. For example, a person who experiences excessive anxiety when approaching strangers at a party, or a public speaking phobic, might call on the assistance of two or three helpers to stand in for guests or an audience. An animal phobic might use a china ornament to represent the dog, cat or other fear-producing creature. An anxious executive might imagine the bedroom to be his office. Use your imagination plus some simple props to help you transform your actual surroundings into the anxiety environment.

Start to talk and behave as you would like to in the real situation. Speak out loud, use the appropriate gestures and put into effect any helpful strategies obtained from Part Three. Watch out for negative thoughts or anxiety and combat them quickly with Positive Self-Talk and Quick Relaxation.

The keynote to success when using this procedure is to *take your time*. Most people with anxiety difficulties are so determined to get difficult situations over and done with, that they rush blindly through them – hoping to succeed by sheer speed and will power. This, of course, simply increases the likelihood of anxiety. So keep all your movements slow and casual. When you feel confident that you are in control of the anxiety in the mock situation, you should move on to practise in real life using the actual anxiety stimulus.

Once again, move slowly, take notice of your surroundings and every now and then stop and relax while standing still and absorbing the details of your environment. An important strategy to use at this stage is the WASP procedure. Each letter in this word stands for one of the basic requirements for the successful use of the Anxiety Antidote:

W – Wait.
A – Absorb.
SP – Slowly Proceed.

When you first enter the real life anxiety-producing situation, do not rush to get out of it.

Wait: Use Differential Relaxation. Bring any unsteadiness in your breathing back under control. Relax your shoulder and facial muscles. Let your arms flop down at your sides. Do not hurry onwards because this will only make you more anxious.

Many people with anxiety difficulties feel embarrassed about doing this in public. They are certain that everybody will stop and stare at them. This is seldom true, since most people are far too busy going about their own affairs to wonder why somebody should be standing still and doing nothing. But if it *does* make you self-conscious, there are plenty of simple strategies which can be used to disguise the fact that you are pausing to relax and take notice of your surroundings. Look in a shop window; study the items of a bus or train; read a poster; or carry a small street directory around with you and pretend to be looking for a road. At the same time, if you have decided to use a biofeedback instrument you could hold onto this in your hand and quickly monitor how rapidly you are relaxing.

Absorb: Look around you. Turn your head slowly while you examine your surroundings. This can be a very rewarding experience. Most of us hurry so quickly from one place to the next that we take in very little of what goes on around us. You will be surprised how much you start to see once you really use your eyes and take the time. Buildings which you thought you knew quite well may reveal interesting new shapes and details. Passers-by will change from an anonymous scurrying crowd into interesting individuals. Even in a big city, you may find unexpected signs of wildlife – birds nesting in the most unusual places, squirrels in nearby parks. Observe your surroundings in as much detail as possible.

Slowly proceed: When you are well relaxed, move on again. Go slowly, absorbing your surroundings as you do so. If you feel anxiety starting to build up then stop again. Use Differential Relaxation to bring down the physical response and the Positive Self-Talk to control any mental confusion.

On your return from such a training trip, be sure to carry out a few minutes of debriefing. Sit down comfortably, relax and go over your performance. In particular, think about how you managed to keep anxiety under control. Note any extra methods which you used beyond those which you planned on using. Then build up yet more Positive Self-Talk, based on how you managed in real life, so that you can feed these into your list of anxiety-reducing statements. Also, be pleased with yourself. Congratulate yourself on the positive aspects of your behaviour – and even, if you wish, give yourself a reward for doing your best. It is important to make your practice worthwhile in this way and you should not think it wrong to bask in your successes, using them to spur you on to the next situation.

Practise each situation in real life several times. Make your Quick Relaxation and Positive Self-Talk more and more refined until they come naturally and easily. When you are confident in your ability to control a particular anxiety situation, move on to the next, but remember to keep practising frequently all the items on the hierarchy list which you have already mastered.

If you get stuck at any point, or if you have difficulties with any of the practice session, do not give up. Go back and practise the last situation with which you felt confident and try to work out additional Positive Self-Talk statements. If you still have difficulty, it is probably because you are trying to take

---

*Summary**

Anxiety Management involves training the body to respond to an initial spurt of anxiety with relaxation rather than with spiralling panic.

Use a loud noise, for example hands clapped sharply together, to produce an initial startle response. Notice the feeling of startle. Usually this will involve a sharp lurching sensation in the pit of the stomach as adrenalin is released. As you experience this startle, immediately relax. After a few days your body will start to respond automatically with feelings of relaxation whenever it experiences a startle.

---

* If you have any difficulty learning the techniques of Positive Self-Talk and Anxiety Management, it may help to send for details of a training programme available on cassette from LIFESKILLS, 3 Brighton Road, London N2 8JU.

Sequence

Relax ⟶ Noise (Startle Response) ⟶ Notice the feelings of Startle ⟶ Relax

Use Anxiety Management and Positive Self-Talk statements to help you deal with situations taken from your graded lists. Start with the lowest and least anxiety-generating situation. Relax and then proceed to imagine the situation as vividly as possible. Use Relaxation and Positive Self-Talk to counter any anxieties which this creates.

When you are able to go through a situation in imagination, practise in real life. First rehearse encounters, using your imagination, props and other people to re-create the anxiety-producing environment.

Finally go out into the actual anxiety situation using Relaxation Positive Self-Talk and WASP to help you. WASP stands for:

WAIT . . . ABSORB . . . SLOWLY PROCEED

It should remind you to move slowly, take in your surroundings and wait whenever you start feeling anxious.

At the end of each attempt, debrief on what you did, said and thought. Use successes to help you construct further Positive Self-Talk statements.

Congratulate yourself and reward all successes.

Practise each situation in your hierarchy list several times until you can carry out the desired activities without anxiety. Then move on to the next situation on your list. But do not neglect to practise the behaviours already dealt with in earlier situations. In this way you will prevent anxiety from recurring.

too big a step at once. Go through the hierarchy list again and see if it is not possible to put in an intermediate situation between the one you can accomplish easily and the one giving you unexpected trouble.

Anxiety Management and Children

Children can be taught Anxiety Management in exactly the same way as adults. Start by carrying out Relaxation training so that the child is free from tension. Then warn them that, at some time during the next ten seconds, you are going to make them jump with a loud noise. Explain that you want them to notice what it feels like to be startled in this way and to see how quickly they can learn to relax. Practise in this way several times during each period of relaxation and the child will begin to control the startle response more and more quickly and easily.

If your child is especially sensitive and might get upset by the loud noise, explain very carefully that you are not trying to frighten or punish in any way. Make a game of it. If you are helping several children, let them see who can relax first after the noise. Alternatively, go through the training with the child lying close beside them, to provide a sense of security.

After a few training sessions, start to show them how to use relaxation in mock anxiety situations. For example, if the child is anxious over some aspect of school life get them to imagine that part of the home is their classroom. Play the role of the teacher or another child. Get them to act out the situation as realistically as possible. Tell them that as soon as they feel anxious they are to relax. Even quite young children are capable of carrying out this type of training. In the *Family and Children* section of Part Three, you will find a number of anxiety-producing situations which can be helped by this form of role-playing combined with anxiety management.

The Antidote and Biofeedback Equipment

Biofeedback is becoming increasingly popular as a means of finding out exactly what is going on inside our bodies. The equipment need not be difficult to operate and many instruments can be bought at moderate prices.

With this type of equipment, it is possible to monitor electrical activity in the brain and in muscles and to detect small increases in anxiety by measuring changes in the electrical conductivity of the skin using a gadget called a galvanic skin response meter. To do this, small electrodes are fastened around the fingers. The machine, which can be adjusted for volume and sensitivity, is turned on and the subject relaxes. As the level of *sympathetic* arousal falls, less sweat is produced and the meter indicates this, either on a dial or by a diminishing buzzing sound. By progressively increasing the sensitivity and then bringing down the pointer or the volume of the sound, a person can become more and more deeply relaxed.

In this relaxed state, anxiety responses so small that one would not normally be aware of them can be detected. For example, the very relaxed subject is asked to imagine that he or she is getting behind the driving wheel of a car. At once, the meter registers a small rise in anxiety. Anticipating a possibly risky or stressful situation, *sympathetic* arousal has been stepped up and this has produced a tiny increase in the amount of sweat being secreted through the pores of the fingers. The sweat has increased the conductivity of the skin and so affected the meter.

Now the subject is told that they are driving down a busy street. In response to this imagined situation, they become even more aroused and this is shown by the meter. Finally, they are told their car has skidded on a wet road into the path of a truck. The meter is now likely to be indicating a very high level of *sympathetic* arousal. Yet if you ask the person whether or not they feel anxious they might often say: 'No, of course not. I am very relaxed.'

Such biofeedback equipment can be used to improve on the

startle trigger which, it can now be seen, occurs at a relatively advanced stage of anxiety, although it is still quite easy at this point to control the response. By monitoring changes in *sympathetic* arousal which are normally too small and subtle to be noticed, one can detect increases in anxiety long before this would otherwise be possible.

Part Three

Strategies for Anxieties

INTRODUCTION

The Antidote, when correctly used, will enable you to control the mental and physical symptoms of anxiety in a swift and effective manner. But it may still be very desirable to reduce the level of anxiety you are currently experiencing. To do this, it will probably be necessary to adopt a different attitude towards major anxiety-producing difficulties by learning and putting into effect a suitable lifestyle strategy. This will allow you to change your approach to stressful situations in such a way that their power to generate anxiety is greatly diminished.

In this part of the book, you will find forty such strategies in the four Life Areas of Social, Sexual, Family and Work situations. These are intended to provide guidance as to the most direct and rapid methods of attaining this new approach to commonly experienced anxiety problems.

It is not claimed that these strategies will provide you with the complete and final answer to major anxiety difficulties. Since no two people have identical problems, it would clearly be impossible to offer a tailor-made solution to each and every anxiety situation. But even if this could be done it would hardly be desirable. We must all develop our own lifestyles and cope with inevitable set-backs and snags in a way best suited to our particular personalities and temperaments. Anybody who tried to work according to the precepts and prejudices of another would be gravely limiting their scope for action and personal initiative. All that can justifiably be claimed for these strategies is that they should provide a sound practical framework on which you can construct your own programmes of change. It is hoped that in some cases they will give you factual information which offers reassurance and perhaps some insight into the origins of a particular difficulty. In some instances, you may feel that the advice is little more than common sense. One can only say in reply to such comments that 'common sense' is often a scarce commodity and the most straightforward and practical way out of a problem can easily be overlooked by an excessively anxious person. The selection of these strategies was guided by experience of the type of anxiety problems raised at social skills training groups, during family therapy sessions, in discussions with industrial and commercial clients as well as in clinical consultations. A further consideration in selecting the anxieties and strategies to be considered here was the need to concentrate on those to which there were the kind of practical answers which:

(1) Lent themselves to a reasonably straightforward and fairly concise description.
(2) Could be safely and satisfactorily put into practice by an anxious reader having to work without the benefit of further consultation or professional guidance.

One or two strategies were also included, which are largely a statement of some basic psychological or biological fact. This has been done because experience shows that considerable anxiety is generated in those who are either ignorant of these facts or, more frequently and damagingly, seriously misinformed. Inevitably, perhaps, such ignorance and misinformation is mainly to be found in the area of sexual anxieties.

Clearly such an approach must be somewhat superficial at times. However, if you use the strategies most appropriate to your current anxiety difficulties, and these you will find by completing the simple thirty statement *Anxiety Analysis* which precedes each of the four Life Areas, you will find sufficient basic facts and strategies either to eliminate your problems or to alleviate them considerably. Remember that these strategies have been designed to work in conjunction with the Antidote. Only by bringing the mental and physical effects of excessive anxiety under control will it be possible to take full advantage of the information contained in this Part of the book.

ANXIETIES INCLUDED IN PART THREE

Life Area One: Social Anxieties

 (1) When holding conversations (page 125).
 (2) When refusing requests (page 133).
 (3) When eating out (page 136).
 (4) When criticised (page 138).
 (5) When travelling on public transport (page 141).
 (6) When feeling angry (page 144).
 (7) When joining social groups (page 147).
 (8) When speaking in public (page 150).
 (9) When asking for a date (page 152).
(10) When bored socially (page 154).

Life Area Two: Sexual Anxieties

 (1) When intimacy arises (page 160).
 (2) When erection difficulties occur (page 164).
 (3) When trying to achieve orgasms (page 167).
 (4) When sexual activity ceases (page 171).
 (5) When masturbating (page 174).
 (6) When sex declines with ageing (page 176).
 (7) When virginity is lost (page 178).
 (8) When going through menopause (page 180).
 (9) When considering physical appearance (page 182).
(10) When confronted with sexual variation (page 184).

Life Area Three: Family Anxieties

 (1) When the baby cries (page 189).
 (2) When children start school (page 192).
 (3) When a child has a fantasy friend (page 196).
 (4) When children wet the bed (page 198).

Life Area Four: Work Anxieties

LIFE AREA ONE
SOCIAL ANXIETIES AND STRATEGIES

Anxiety Analysis

In order to help you find out which of the strategies in th
section are likely to prove the most helpful read through th
thirty statements in the Anxiety Analysis below and no
the numbers of any which are applicable to your currer
difficulties. Then refer to the Answer Chart which will direct yo
to the appropriate strategies in this, and possibly other, Li
Areas as well.

Anxiety Analysis Inventory

(1) I become anxious when I have to say 'no' in a soci
situation.
(2) I am anxious in social situations because I find it difficu
to talk to people.
(3) I become anxious when I am criticised.
(4) I become anxious when I feel angry at anybody.
(5) I am anxious when I think about going to parties.
(6) I become anxious in intimate situations.
(7) I am anxious when I meet strangers.
(8) I am anxious if I am asked to speak in public.
(9) I become anxious if I have to travel on public transport.
(10) I become anxious when I try to make friends.
(11) I become anxious when I am holding a conversation.
(12) I become anxious when I try to break into a group
people at a party.
(13) I am anxious because my life seems so empty and borin
(14) I become anxious if I lose my temper with somebody.
(15) I become anxious if I have to hold the floor during
conversation.

(16) I become anxious when I am asked to eat with strangers present.

(17) I become anxious if I am unjustly attacked.

(18) I become anxious when taking part in a conversation because I think what I have to say will sound stupid.

(19) I become anxious if I am asked to a restaurant.

(20) I become anxious when I am alone with a member of the opposite sex.

(21) I become anxious when I talk to a group of people.

(22) I become anxious when I have to ask somebody for a date.

(23) I become anxious when talking because I am afraid I may 'dry up' when telling a story.

(24) I become anxious when I learn that somebody has insulted me.

(25) I become anxious in a social situation because I am sure people must find me boring.

(26) I become anxious in public because I think I am afraid that I will make a fool of myself.

(27) I become anxious when I think about how little I am doing with my life.

(28) I become anxious when I try to talk to a member of the opposite sex.

(29) I become anxious when flying on holiday.

(30) I become anxious if I think that people are talking about me.

Answer Chart

Statements Ticked	Most Appropriate Strategies (S)
2, 11, 12, 15, 18, 23, 25, 28	S. One (Social) S. Five (Family) S. Six (Work)
1	S. Two (Social) S. Ten (Sexual) S. Five (Family) S. Two (Work)
16, 19	S. Three (Social)
3, 17, 24, 30	S. Four (Social) S. Nine (Sexual) S. Four (Work)
9, 29	S. Five (Social) S. Six (Family) S. Eight (Family)
4, 14	S. Six (Social) S. Nine (Family) S. Two (Work) S. Eight (Work)
5, 7, 12	S. Seven (Social) S. Seven (Family)
8, 21, 26	S. Eight (Social) S. Six (Work) S. Nine (Work) S. Ten (Work)
6, 10, 20, 22, 28	S. Nine (Social) S. Nine (Sexual) S. Three (Work) S. Nine (Work)
13, 27	S. One (Social) S. Seven (Social) S. Ten (Social)

STRATEGY ONE

Anxieties – When Holding Conversations

The main problem which faces most people who have conversation difficulties is being excessively concerned as to whether or not they are making a good impression and saying the right thing. Instead of listening attentively to the other person and then letting their contribution flow naturally from what has been said, their brains are busy with thoughts such as: 'What will I say when he stops talking' or 'Dare I really express my opinion on this to her?' Because the mental processes are so cluttered with worried thoughts about how the performance will appear, scant attention is paid to what the other person is actually saying. Accordingly, when the person who has been talking comes to an end of what they have to say for the time being, the anxious listener is left fumbling for words.

Similarly, when the anxious conversationalist is talking, the thought will often arise: 'What am I going to say next?' or 'Does what I am talking about sound stupid to the other people?' In the middle of telling a story or expressing an opinion, they may begin to falter, lose the thread of what they are saying or dry up completely.

Strategies

Positive strategies which help greatly for both the 'listening' and 'talking' aspects of conversation can be learned by practising with a co-operative friend. The main rules to observe for effective conversation are that when you are listening to another person you should process what they are saying in a mentally and verbally *active* fashion. This will make the information clearer and more useful to you in your own conversation and encourage the person who is talking to continue to do so. When talking, it is important to concentrate primarily on the points which you have to make and only secondarily on what other people may be thinking about you. This is not to say that you should ignore cues and comments from others but you should not make the mistake of shaping everything which you say into some preconceived idea of what is being expected of you. To do so will inevitably produce a boring and ingratiating delivery that contributes nothing to the conversation. The basic skills which you should practise with your helper, in order to achieve a good conversational ability, can be divided into speaker or 'sender' skills and listener or 'receiver' skills. Since most people find 'receiver' skills easier to develop initially, let us begin with these.

(1) *Recognition Training:* Frequently, people who are unsure of how to respond to another person's comments will simply look blankly back or murmur a non-committal: 'uh-huh'. This can be disconcerting for the *sender*, as he or she will not know whether the opinion or information has got through. When listening to information which is factual or fairly trivial in content, such as comments about the weather, an actual verbal acknowledgement is required from the receiver. There is no need to make it lengthy but simply a polite recognition of the other person's contribution. For example:

SENDER: 'The traffic was really heavy this morning.'
RECEIVER: 'Yes, it's not usually this congested.'

or:

SENDER: 'I hear that Fred Jones is retiring.'
RECEIVER: 'Oh, really. I always thought he would go on forever.'

But it is important not to pretend to understand if you do not. For example:

SENDER: 'Isn't that report about bribery in big business a disgrace?'
RECEIVER: 'Really? I didn't see that on the news.'

A recognition comeback such as this is then likely to produce a piece of information which you might otherwise not have heard about and you can simply listen while the sender delivers it.

You can practise this skill with a friend, using a light-hearted though very helpful exercise in which, for periods of about ten minutes you simply take it in turns to be a 'sender' and a 'recognition' receiver. The statements which each of you send in turn need not be in any way related to one another. The sole object of this exercise is to introduce as many different topics as possible so that the number of ways of recognising are as varied as you can make them. For example one section of such a practice interchange might go like this:

A. 'My puppy really won't learn not to make a mess in the house.'
B. 'Dogs really can be a problem. I understand they are closing down the local library.'
A. 'What a shame; it gave a lot of people great pleasure. I hear they are going for a Mars landing in two years time.'
B. 'Really – that must cost a fantastic amount. I'm going to spend the weekend digging over my garden.'
A. 'That sounds like hard work. There have been a lot of redundancies in my office recently.'

And so on. It is not necessary to go into long explanations of your reactions or comments but simply to keep the exchange at a casual and flowing level.

Empathic Listening: Empathy is what we show when we are trying to share the feelings of the person to whom we are speaking. In other words, when we try to get under their skin emotionally. This form of responding is of particular importance when the conversation is of a more intimate nature and deep feelings and opinions on issues are being expressed. Such feelings may be ones of sadness or irritation or they may be joyful and lighthearted. In essence, the skill is to extract from what the sender has said the two major components of *facts* and the *feelings* behind the facts and send back a version of what they have just said in your own words. When you first begin to learn this skill, it may seem a little artificial – as though you are simply echoing their own attitudes. But, with practice, you can make your empathic statement sufficiently different so that it reflects their feelings and leads to a response on their part of the type: 'Yes, you've really hit it there. That's exactly how I feel.'

Again, you can practise this with a friend, who should be instructed to talk about something which has recently made them feel some strong emotion but to tell you about it in such a way that you have a chance, about every two sentences or so, to make an empathic reply. A conversation may go like this:

A. 'I had a fantastic day yesterday. My boyfriend surprised me by meeting me from work and taking me out to dinner.'

B. 'How marvellous! It was lovely of him to think of that.'

A. 'Yes, wasn't it. We went to the Trattoria in the High Street and the service was so good and the waiters were so attentive.'

B. 'The Trattoria does look like a nice restaurant. It's always so pleasant when there is a good atmosphere.'

A. 'Isn't it. Mind you we had to walk about three blocks to get a taxi after we left and it was raining.'

B. 'Oh, what a shame. But that sounds a small price to pay for such a good night out.'
– and so on.

You can see from the above responses that they take a little more effort than just murmuring: 'Oh, really . . . how nice . . . what fun' and other trite responses. But by verbalising the answers in such a way, you are proving to the sender that you have not only listened to what they are saying but are sharing in their feelings about it also. Similar responses can be made for any kind of emotional statement. Do not feel that you are putting on a mask or being insincere when carrying out empathic listening. You are simply becoming more sensitive to what others are saying.

(3) *Questioning:* When you are experiencing difficulties, it is often tempting to be drawn into a cross-examination of the person who is talking, firing question after question at them in order to keep them involved. But such a tactic can be very oppressive for the person who is talking and should be used carefully and sparingly in conversation. Notice that with empathic listening there were no direct questions but simply return statements which gave the impression to the sender that they were being interesting and that the receiver would like them to continue for a while in a similar way. However, if you are going to use questions occasionally, try to make them easy to answer rather than a blunt 'Why?' 'Did he?' 'Is it really?'. Instead try to lead a little with your questions. This is a skill you should also practise with your friend. For example:

A. 'I went hill walking last weekend for the first time in three years.'
B. 'Goodness, didn't you get awfully tired?'
A. 'Yes, I ached a bit on the Sunday but I soon walked it off. It felt absolutely marvellous after all this time.'

B. 'It must have been. What sort of things did you go there particularly to see?'

A. 'Well I am especially keen on landscape photography and there were so many picture opportunities in that area.'

B. 'I didn't know you were keen on photography as well. Did you teach yourself or did you join a camera club?'

– and so on.

Using these three skills, you will find it already very much easier to converse in all kinds of situations and as you practise them you will discover that you can use a mixture of these three basic receiver skills to stimulate the conversation.

Now let us look at some sender skills. These too should be practised with your friend.

(1) *Self-Disclosure:* If you have difficulty in talking about yourself, your feelings, hopes or opinions, practise doing this with a friend and noticing how it feels to use the personal pronoun rather than edging around your own point-of-view. Many people use the word: 'One. . . .' to avoid talking about themselves. For example: 'When one gets into a situation like this it is very hard for one to know what to do.' What is actually being said here is: 'I am in a jam and need help!' The best way to practise self-disclosure is to become the sender in the empathic listening exercise described above. The rules are that you must talk only about *your* personal feelings and opinions on various matters and not in any way hedge your bets just in case the other person disagrees. State your position firmly and stick to it, even though you feel the other person may be at variance with you.

(2) *Holding the Floor:* For the person who has difficulty in talking at length, there is nothing more anxiety-producing than to be asked: 'Go on then, tell us how it all happened!'

or 'Well, tell us how you see that taking place over the next few years!' – in other words being given a clear invitation to speak at length for a few minutes about a particular subject. The rule here is to ignore how your performance seems to the other people present. The pause – which is a nightmare to most anxious speakers – should be used to full effect. Do not be afraid to start off your remarks by saying: 'Let me think back for a few seconds' or 'Well, it's not too well thought out in my mind at the moment and I may hesitate a little but I will try to explain.' In this way, you are making it clear to your listeners that you are being asked to do something quite difficult and they must bear with you if your delivery is not perfect. If you tell them this they will, in most cases, prove completely co-operative and understanding.

Do not ruin a good story for the sake of pedantic accuracy. There is nothing worse than having to listen to an anecdote or description which involves constant backtracking to correct unimportant points of detail. Most of us have been subjected to rambling stories of the type: 'I left home at 7.15 to catch the train, well it might have been nearer 7.25 I suppose. Anyhow it was raining, no wait a minute it was fine when I left the house but started to rain when I reached the corner. . . .' Keep the flow steady even though there may be the occasional inaccuracies. Only trouble to correct major errors of fact which are relevant to your account.

(3) *Exit Skills:* Having held the floor for some time you should take care not to overdo your privileged position and, by watching to see whether anyone else is trying to make a contribution, decide on a certain point at which to stop sending and begin receiving again. This is usually done by winding up with some comment like: 'But tell me, Anne, didn't you have a similar experience recently?' Here you are signalling both your intention to close your own period of sending and your wish for somebody else to take over. Resist the temptation to talk on for the sake of it and make

a clean break in the conversation so that your intentions are clear.

Use Differential Relaxation while practising and actually using all these skills and you will soon find that your difficulties and anxieties are eliminated.

STRATEGY TWO

Anxieties – When Refusing Requests

Saying 'no' is often one of the most difficult and anxiety-producing things we have to do. Many people feel so guilty about refusing a request, no matter how inconvenient and unreasonable it may be, that they either agree or go through an elaborate pretence to avoid a flat refusal: 'I would really like to go out with you next week, but I have to work late at the office and then there is the phone call I may have to wait in for. . . .' We have probably all used such excuses at times to prevent us having to make use of the simpler but, apparently, more brutal alternative of just saying 'no'. Yet we all have a perfect right to decline to do anything which we do not want to do and should never feel the need to defend ourselves elaborately when we wish to turn down an invitation, decline a request or refuse a proposition of some kind.

Strategies

The easiest way of saying 'no' is to do just that. It is direct, honest, unambiguous and unmistakable. Using a softer form of refusal may be easier initially but it leaves the door open for further discussion. If you say for example: 'I am not sure that will be possible.' Then the persuasive person will come back with a whole set of 'convincing' reasons why it really is, or ought to be, possible. They can build up the pressure and work on your obvious reluctance to give offence. This type of emotional blackmail is not only distressing but may be all too successful in persuading you to agree to something against your will or better judgement. A firm 'no', provided it is repeated two or three times, will make it clear to the most persistent and manipulative individual that you really will not go along with their demands. Further, remember that an assertive response not only states your position unequivocally but might also give information to the other person which prevents similar unwelcome demands being made again. It might even teach that person something, as in the following example:

A. 'But it seems so sensible for you to come on holiday with us.'
B. 'Well my answer to that has to be "no", although I do want to thank you for inviting me. However, I think that while we get on very well in limited social situations, an extended period together would, I feel, stretch our relationship to breaking point.'

This may seem a very blunt and even unkind refusal, but if it honestly expresses a feeling about the relationship, it prevents the other person building up any false hopes or expectations. In the long term, it is far kinder to say what you really feel than to hedge and prevaricate.

Fears about what other people will say to you, or think about you, if you tell the truth are frequently the cause of an inability to refuse a request. But remember that people who constantly say 'yes' when they really want to say 'no' often put themselves and others into impossibly difficult situations. Unable to turn down a request until the last minute, they will then invent some illness, office commitment or unexpected guest as an excuse for not doing what was expected of them. In this way, they will simply lose the respect and co-operation of others in the long term.

The ability to say 'no' and stick to it is something which has to be learned. Practise this with a friend or member of the family. Ask them to be as insistent and manipulative as they can be while you simply stick to your guns and reiterate 'No, it is not possible,' without allowing yourself to be drawn into all sorts of real or imagined excuses.

Use the Antidote to help you control the physical symptoms

of anxiety which such direct refusal may generate in the early stages. Later, however, your own command of these situations will remove any anxiety you may once have felt. Remember that by avoiding the immediate anxiety which may be produced by a refusal, you will reinforce the 'playing for time' or 'ambiguous' type of response thereby making it that much harder to say 'no' in the future.

STRATEGY THREE

Anxieties – When Eating Out

Anxieties produced when eating with strangers, in restaurants, canteens or even at home are the result of a fairly common phobic difficulty. Such a phobia can develop over a period of time or strike quickly and unexpectedly for no apparent reason. Escape and avoidance responses then rapidly establish it through *negative reinforcement*.

Strategies

Learn the Antidote skills thoroughly and make up a graded list of difficult situations as described in Part Two. A typical hierarchy list for this type of phobia might read as follows:

(1) Eating at home with stranger present.
(2) Eating alone at table in restaurant near exit.
(3) Eating alone in secluded table when restaurant is crowded.
(4) Eating at table in restaurant with one other person.
(5) Eating at table with group of people.

Go through this list using mental imagery. Make the scene as vivid as possible. Do not only picture the surroundings but try to smell and taste the food as well. Use the Antidote to prevent yourself from feeling anxious.

When you have gone through each situation a number of times in imagination, practise in real life. Remember WASP. Do not rush through your food without tasting it. Eat slowly. Put down your knife and fork between mouthfuls and chew the food thoroughly. Taste it and feel the texture of it in your mouth. After a few mouthfuls look around you. Absorb the details of the room in which you are eating. Look at other diners. Work slowly through the graded list. Do not rush it, but make sure you have one situation under control before proceeding to the next.

As digestion is one of the activities which stimulates the *parasympathetic* branch of the autonomic nervous system, the mere act of eating, chewing, swallowing and processing the food will tend to bring down the anxiety-producing *sympathetic* response.

When you have completed the programme, you should find it quite easy to eat in public without any anxiety. But, at least in the short term, you may not derive as much pleasure as previously from the activity. In that case, use the Emotional Training procedure described at the end of Part Two to help you reintroduce this enjoyment during the transitional period following the removal of the anxiety and the spontaneous feelings of pleasure produced by the activity itself.

STRATEGY FOUR

Anxieties – When Criticised

Many people find it hard to accept criticism, whether or not it is justified and may become extremely anxious if they learn that they have been adversely commented on behind their backs. The confident person may take it as a slur, the under-confident is likely to see it as confirmation of their failings. Neither response is especially helpful. If the criticism is constructive and justified then you might derive considerable benefit by following the advice which has been given. If it is merely malicious and pointless then it is best to be able to dismiss it from your mind without further consideration.

Strategies

When considering criticism we must look at the two main components of any critical comment:

(1) The actual opinion being expressed at a factual level.
(2) The manner and tone in which it was delivered.

Justified Criticism: If you judge a criticism to be justified then the most appropriate and useful type of response is to say words to the effect: 'Yes, I think you have made a very good point there and I had not considered it before. It would be certainly worth my while to try to incorporate it into my way of running things.' There is no need to feel with such a response that you have lost face or that you are inferior. It simply shows that you are able to change your behaviour for the better and capitalise on feedback.

Unjustified Criticism: If you feel strongly that you have been misunderstood or attacked for no good reason, then you should make a direct statement to the effect: 'I think that is a quite unnecessary and inappropriate comment on my abilities and from my point-of-view it is perfectly clear that you have misunderstood the true situation. I will go over it with you should you wish to correct any misunderstandings but I certainly think you should reassess your opinions.'

You must also realise that you have a perfect right to disregard the comments completely, whether they are justified or unfair, helpful or malicious.

Consider the criticism seriously before making any reply or deciding that it should be ignored. Do not rush into an angry exchange which will serve no constructive purpose. Use the WASP procedure as detailed in Part Two. *Wait* a moment while you reflect on what has been said. *Absorb* the two components on the comment. What facts have you been given to work on? Are they correct or incorrect? What sort of tone or manner of delivery was used? This will provide a major clue as to the motives of the person who offered the criticism. Was it a point-scoring tactic designed to make you feel small or put you in the wrong? Was it a stupid retort blurted out in anger or from a sense of irritation? When you have decided on the best course of action, whether that is to deny or to accept the criticism, *Slowly Proceed* to reply with a defence or rebuttal or simply to shrug it off.

If there is a certain truth in what has been said, but you object to the sarcastic or harsh way in which the criticism was delivered, then make your views clear. Use Differential Relaxation to help you stay cool, calm and collected both while considering the criticism and when replying.

You will find it very helpful if you practise these skills with a friend in a role-playing situation and in real life. Set up rehearsal sessions in which your friend offers various types of criticism, some valid and justified, some ridiculous and merely unhelpful. Respond and then assess how well or badly you did. If you feel you failed to answer the criticisms effectively, think about how you might have improved your performance. It will also be helpful to go through critical exchanges in your imagination. Mental rehearsal of this kind is especially valuable if you know that you will be going into an encounter where criticism is to be expected.

STRATEGY FIVE

Anxieties – When Travelling on Public Transport

Anxiety about travelling on public transport is frequently due to a phobic response. Part of the difficulty can be the fear that something will happen to make the person look or feel foolish. There is often a belief that people are watching and will be mocking if anything goes wrong. There may be strong physical symptoms such as sweating, trembling, a feeling of nausea, blushing and faintness which increase the mental anguish centred around loss of control and subsequent ridicule.

Strategies

Learn the Antidote procedure thoroughly, as the ability to overcome physical anxiety symptoms will go a long way towards reducing mental anxiety. Develop sound Positive Self-Talk statements based on recent experiences or on any memories you may have of times when you managed well by employing some tactic, for example by sitting near the exit. Incorporate these into your mental imagery training as described in Part Two. When constructing your graded list, make sure that each situation only involves a small increase in the amount of anxiety present. For example, some people might find it too great a jump to go from:

(1) Sitting in bus near exit.   Increased Anxiety
(2) Sitting in front of crowded bus.

With the first situation brought under control using the Antidote, they might attempt the next situation on the graded list and fail because it was actually much further up their hierarchy of fears than they had believed. A revised list might look as follows:

(1) Sitting in bus near exit.
(2) Sitting a few seats away from exit in fairly empty bus.
(3) Sitting a few seats from exit in busy bus.   Increased Anxiety
(4) Sitting in front of bus which is not crowded.
(5) Sitting in front of crowded bus.

If it even proves difficult to control the anxiety when attempting a new situation, the answer is almost always that the graded list has been incorrectly constructed. Revise the list and go through the new situations in imagination before attempting them in real life. Remember that you may have to devote several sessions to Mental Imagery training before setting out to tackle the problem in reality.

When going through the actual situation do not forget WASP. Never rush. Absorb the details of your surrounds and Slowly Proceed. Take your time and use Quick and Differential Relaxation to bring anxiety symptoms under control.

After each session, debrief on how you got on. Do not be depressed if it proved more difficult than you anticipated or if you failed to accomplish all you had hoped for. You are attempting to change a major piece of behaviour which has probably become very firmly established through Negative Reinforcement after a long period of avoidance and escape responses. Such a behavioural change must inevitably take time and effort. Extract all the positive aspects of each practice session and build them into your next set of Positive Self-Talk statements. Never allow these statements to become unrealistic or any failure will generate negative comments. Do not say: 'I am going to succeed . . .' rather tell yourself that: 'It is going to be rather tricky but I will manage better if I. . . .'

When you have carried out a training session, reward yourself. Give yourself a small present, take some time off to enjoy a cup of tea or coffee, spend some time talking to a friend on the 'phone. Positive reinforcers like this help to establish the new and desired behaviour quickly and effectively.

When you have managed to deal with all the situations in your graded list, start practising for things going wrong. For example, you may be anxious about doing something which will attract attention, such as dropping your change on the floor, not being able to find your briefcase or handbag, holding up a queue of people and so on. The way to eliminate these anxieties is to do something which deliberately attracts attention to yourself. For example, you might offer a note for the fare and then count the change very carefully, ask a fellow passenger to tell you when you reach a destination, talk to the conductor about the route, drop some money on the floor and so on. These pieces of behaviour will probably make you slightly anxious but you will find that you can quite easily control the response using the Antidote. The purpose of this training is to prevent some small incident like this occurring without prior rehearsal and making you suddenly very anxious again. If and when such an incident occurs by mistake, you will be ready for it. When you practise this type of situation still use WASP. Do not rush to sort the problem out. Absorb your surroundings and study the reactions of your fellow passengers.

STRATEGY SIX

Anxieties – When Feeling Angry

Anxiety about feeling anger towards somebody can often lead to a building up of irritation and tension which keeps the person on edge for days or weeks. They may then explode with rage completely inappropriately against people who have done nothing to justify their wrath. The business man who takes a dispute with his superiors out on his wife and the mother who is furious with her children because she has been served by a rude store assistant are typical examples of this diverted rage response. Suppression of anger in the appropriate circumstances is usually due to two main anxieties. The first is worry over how those responsible for the anger will react. Will they become very angry and perhaps violent themselves? Will they simply think less well of you as a result of the outburst? The second fear is that it may not be possible to control one's anger once it has been unleashed. People who are unfamiliar with this type of emotion are often convinced that they will become 'blind with rage' and do or say something which they will greatly regret once their temper has cooled. In fact, it is much more likely that the man or woman who is constantly repressing feelings of anger will one day lose control rather than the person who knows how to handle these emotions as a result of training and practice. The meek-mannered husband who was mutely patient with his nagging wife for twenty years and then buried a meat cleaver in her head is not exactly an unfamiliar figure in criminal history. In fact, the majority of murders take place in the home and involve people who have lived together for years with 'never an angry word' between them.

Strategies

Anger is only an explosive force if it is allowed to build up under pressure but being able to lose your temper in a controlled manner can be learned. The main rule is that you should always express anger at the time and in the context to which it is appropriate. Suppressed rage always creates anxieties, either by being diverted onto innocent parties – which often leads to feelings of guilt and repentence later – or by being absorbed.

When expressing anger, it is not necessary to use clever, cutting remarks. You should simply make clear your annoyance at the other person's attitude or conduct. This is all that is needed to state your position assertively while providing the other person with valuable feedback as to your true feelings. Such a response will certainly not make other people think any less well of you. Indeed, it will probably increase their respect when they find that you are willing and able to defend yourself. In situations where you feel that a display of anger is necessary and would be beneficial, allow yourself to externalise the feeling physically and vocally. Thump the table, stamp your foot, raise your voice or take any other action which helps you express your rage. This type of physical expression of fury is especially helpful if you are one of those people who find it very difficult to become angry. Simply by *'acting'* in an enraged way you will *become* enraged. You will also discover that as your anger increases, the anxiety symptoms you may have experienced when contemplating anger decrease dramatically. This is because an anger response is as effective as relaxation in reducing the *sympathetic* arousal which has been responsible for the symptoms in the first place. In some situations, it is just as appropriate to learn how to become angry in order to control anxiety as it is to be able to relax.

You can train yourself to express anger by a series of simple exercises. It will be necessary to find a friend or relative to help you in this:

1. Anger by numbers

In this exercise, the two of you have a stand-up row using numbers rather than words. The purpose of this is to enable you to shout in a variety of angry ways without the subjective overtones attached to words and sentences. Take it in turns to yell any number at one another and put as much feeling and anger into each word you shout as possible.

2. 'Give me the towel'

In this exercise, each of you takes hold of an end of a towel and you begin shouting angrily at one another: 'Give me the towel' and tugging at it. This exercise helps to increase the bodily expression of anger through the muscle tension associated with vigorous exercise. Really pull at the towel and yell with as much power and feeling as possible: 'Give me the towel.'

3. Insults and Abuse

In this exercise, you hurl abuse at one another, taking it in turn to shout insults of the type: 'You stupid imbecile . . . you make me sick . . . I hate your attitude . . . I can't stand you.' Carry on for five or ten minutes and put as much feeling as possible into the session. Do not worry that this sort of exercise will produce difficulties between you after the event. The fact that it has been clearly set up as an artificial role-playing situation ritualises it to a point where it cannot be taken as a serious confrontation.

These three exercises should be practised regularly together with the strategies described in Strategy Nine (Family).

STRATEGY SEVEN

Anxieties – When Joining Social Groups

To anybody who suffers anxiety in social situations, parties and similar gatherings can present a bewildering scene. Groups and pairings are ever-changing and seem to form and reform in a continuous movement of bodies as people circulate, chat and move on again. The ease with which some guests attach themselves to and become temporarily involved with different groups is often a matter of surprise and envy to the socially anxious. They seem to do it so easily and gracefully; slipping in and out of conversations with no apparent effort while the anxious individual hovers and hesitates as each new opportunity presents itself. At some point, physical anxiety may make the whole situation even worse, leading to eventual withdrawal from yet another social gathering. As we saw in the case history of Phyllis in Part One, when the next invitation is received, memories of the difficulties previously experienced in the party situation may cause it to be declined. In time, such invitations will be few and far between and the anxious person's social life is likely to be very restricted.

Strategies

Learning to interact at a social level in party situations can be achieved by mastering a series of quite definable skills.

1. Non-Demand Observation: First decide to go along to some parties in order to examine, in an objective and non-envious way, the actual mechanics of interchanges between various groups. You will notice several major methods and techniques in use. Some people stand just on the edge of a group for a few seconds, listening to the conversation, and then break into the group by verbal means, sometimes through empathic listening (see Strategy One (Social)) or sometimes by self-disclosure methods as they begin to recount one of their own experiences or opinions. Others may not hesitate, but approach the group with physical gestures such as touching one of the existing group members on the arm or shoulder to attract their attention and thereby slip into the group. Yet others may break into the group conversation by asking whether anyone wants a drink or food or by requesting a light for their cigarette. Different individuals will tend to favour different styles, although these styles will vary from situation to situation. Sometimes, mixtures of techniques will be used. Unless you look for them, however, these basic elements of entering groups may well be missed. During these periods, you should decide quite categorically that you are *not* going to bother about moving into social groups yourself. Simply watch and see whether any of the tactics which other people use can be incorporated into your own repertoire.

2. *Setting Social Goals:* Now begin to go to party situations with quite clearly defined goals as to why you are going. Initially, you will find that a useful goal to adopt is simply to make an entrance into as many groupings of people as you can during the party. Do not be too concerned with any other goals at this time. As you become more competent in joining different groupings, these goals, which may include making dates or entering into arguments or discussions, can develop easily and naturally. Initially, just enjoy approaching and entering groups.

3. *Exit Skills:* Usually, it is quite easy to leave a group or pairing which you have entered. A phrase such as: 'Excuse me, I must go and see where "X" has got to' or 'It's been very interesting talking to you – I hope we meet again later' combined with a simultaneous turning away of the body and gesture with the hand and face signifying farewell for the moment, will leave the others satisfied with the interaction.

With the inevitable party bore, this form of exit may not be strong enough. But unless you have come to the party with the express intention of befriending the most boring person present, a satisfactory method of breaking the connection must be adopted. The only effective way of doing this is to be firm. Say clearly that you have to go over and talk to so-and-so. Having stated this fact, leave without giving the bore a chance to interrupt with something like: 'Yes, of course. But just let me tell you about. . . .' Smile politely and turn away at once. If the person appears to be following you, it is possible to 'plant' him or her on the spot by using the appropriate piece of body language. With a half serious fending off movement place one hand on the person's shoulder, say you must really go and depart. By the time the bore recovers, it will be too late to rejoin you in your next grouping. This might sound rather rude but it may be the only alternative to being stuck with somebody you find dull and uncongenial for the rest of the evening. You have every right to assert your desire to interact with anybody you choose and if you fail to act assertively, the evening is likely to drag along and you will go home feeling depressed and bored.

Use the Antidote to help you control mental and physical anxiety symptoms. Differential Relaxation is especially valuable in social situations. Rehearse group entry and exit skills in your imagination and, if you can find willing helpers, in practical training sessions, with your relatives and friends role-playing the part of the other guests.

STRATEGY EIGHT

Anxieties – When Speaking in Public

Anxieties about speaking in public are common. At a controlled level, a certain amount of *sympathetic* arousal is desirable, since it keys up mind and body to give the best performance. But if this level rises too sharply, it can cause mental confusion and, in extreme cases, give rise to such severe anxiety symptoms, that it proves impossible for the person to continue.

Strategies

The major point to consider when delivering a talk or speech is whether you have covered most of the eventualities through adequate preparation. Only if you are absolutely positive of your abilities should you work without any notes at all and deliver a completely extemporised speech. In most cases, you will need notes on at least main headings to ensure that you deliver the material in a coherent and enjoyable form. Keep these notes as brief as possible and write them on separate cards or small pieces of paper so that they are easy to hold and follow. If you think that it is going to be a difficult delivery, then make your notes fuller so that if you get stuck you know that you can refer to them and get out of trouble. At any point during your speech, when you have either got stuck for some reason, want to refer to your notes or have been asked a question you cannot immediately answer, make it quite clear to your listeners that there will be a short delay while you regain your thoughts. Actually say words to the effect: 'Now just let me gather my thoughts on this before proceeding', and 'I will have to consider that point for a few moments before answering so please bear with me.'

In short, do not worry about pausing. Do not rush on and

become even more flustered. Remember WASP. While you are waiting, use the time to recover your thoughts and combat any anxiety with Differential Relaxation.

Audiences like to feel that you are personally involved with each one of them and the only way a speaker has of doing this effectively is by using eye-contact. You should avoid looking either at no one or at one person exclusively. Both these approaches will prove embarrassing. Try instead to let your eyes travel slowly across your audience at approximately eye level. Flick your eyes from one person to the next, giving each a little share of your eye-contact. You need not do this continuously, as on occasions you may be pointing to a blackboard or visual aids or possibly pacing the platform, if that is your style. Do not overdo such movements as these, however, can easily become distracting and annoying.

The one situation where eye-contact is impossible is when you are writing on a blackboard. While you are doing this, do not try to speak but instead use it as a pause period and then turn around and explain the point on the board to your audience while facing them.

If you are very anxious about speaking in public but have to do it, perhaps as part of your job, it will be helpful if you rehearse in front of a small and friendly audience to start off with. Ask your friends and relatives to help you here. Remember, too, that the more you speak in public the easier it becomes; so once you have started, take every opportunity to practise until the anxiety has disappeared.

STRATEGY NINE

Anxieties – When Asking for a Date

The main reason for anxiety when asking somebody for a date or when trying to make new friends is a fear of rejection. This can lead to an avoidance of those pieces of behaviour necessary to make dates and find friends. The conversation is never allowed to get onto an intimate level, people are kept at arm's length, the vital questions which could lead to a development of the relationship remain unasked. This avoidance is *negatively reinforced* by the reduction of anxiety which it produces. In time, avoidance becomes the normal response but instead of leading to a long-term reduction in anxieties it usually makes them worse as the person becomes lonely, bored and depressed.

Strategies

The important thing to realise, and practise, is that *making the approach matters more than the response of the other person.* If you never ask, you will never be rejected. If you do ask there are bound to be occasions when the other person turns you down. But there will also be many positive responses.

The goal towards which you should be working is not the *acceptance* of an approach but the *approach* itself. You should measure your success not in terms of the number of new relationships which you develop or the dates you get but on the number of approaches you make. You can never do more than let it be known that you are interested. If the other person is also interested, he or she will probably respond in a positive fashion. If they are not interested, they may also make this clear, although you will find it useful to coax and persuade before finally admitting defeat.

It is very important not to take a refusal personally. People can say 'no' for a number of reasons which have nothing to do with any inadequacies on your part. Do not allow a rejection to harm your self-image. On the other hand, if there are a number of refusals it will be useful to consider the reasons why. Perhaps your approach is too timid or ambiguous. Are you really making your intentions clear or leaving it to the other person to read the correct meaning into a rather vague and veiled invitation? Read Strategies One and Seven in this Life Area to help you with your conversation and party skills. If you are turned down, try and find out why. There is no need to demand the information in an aggressive or sulky manner – indeed, such an approach will almost certainly be counter-productive. Simply ask if there is any reason for the person's saying 'no'. Feedback like could well be very useful in modifying your approach on subsequent occasions.

The Antidote will help eliminate the mental and physical anxiety responses which may currently be causing you problems. Use mental imagery rehearsal to improve your approach skills.

If your main problem is in asking for dates, it may be that there are sexual anxieties involved. You should go through the Anxiety Analysis in the next section to help you pin-point possible sources of difficulty.

STRATEGY TEN

Anxieties – When I am Bored Socially

Boredom can produce a number of anxieties. There may be fear that life is slipping past with nothing being achieved, worry that you are wasting your talents in unstimulating activities or surroundings, and concern that you will never be able to break out of what seems to be a dreary lifestyle. One of the main problems with boredom is that it saps the will for change. A bored person can all too easily become apathetic, accepting the changeless nature of the daily routine with the excuse that 'something will be done about it someday'. Strange though it may seem, a very boring existence is sometimes regarded as preferable to the alternative of change and challenge which is seen as anxiety-producing. In this way, boredom is *negatively* reinforced by the avoidance of these anxieties.

Strategies

The first thing to decide is whether you really want change and, if so, how much change will you want to handle? Is your life-style so unstimulating and depressing that you would willingly reject it completely in favour of something more exciting. Or are you going to be happy if you simply inject high points into the weekly routine? Examine your expectations and self-image to see how many negative components they contain. Are you setting your goals unrealistically low or are there elements in your self-image, for example, a lack of confidence or a low opinion of your intelligence or abilities, which are preventing you from seeking out fresh interests.

It is important to bear in mind that boredom is the natural state of mankind. We can only prevent ourselves from becoming bored by doing things which provide us with rewards or positive pay-offs. A person who describes his or her life as being deathly dull is really saying that they have a lack of such pay-offs.

The only way to change the situation is by going out and working at the problem. Life will never alter if you sit around at home worrying over how boring it is.

The first thing to decide is whether you are being held back by negative self-image components. Do you lack certain social skills, such as the ability to make conversation, go to parties or develop new friends? If this is one of your problems, then Strategies One, Seven and Nine in this section of the book should help. If you have sexual problems, then read the next section.

Do not allow yourself to adopt, or be talked into, the: 'I know I cannot do it because I have never tried it or because I am told I couldn't do it' approach to life. If you want to paint pictures but have held back because you worry that you lack sufficient talent, go ahead and paint them – how well or badly is much less important than the pleasure you attain from the activity. If you want to start an active pursuit but feel you are too old, take advice from experts and find out if it is really true or whether you have not simply persuaded yourself that it must be true. Never avoid doing something because you are worried about what other people will think of you.

The second task is to assess your expectations to see if they have been pitched too low. Have you only tackled social situations or hobbies where you were certain to succeed? There is very little positive pay-off in doing something which you know you can do easily and with minimal effort. You should always pitch your expectations just that little bit higher than you consider possible. It is not only better to fail gloriously than to succeed miserably, it is also a far more effective method of banishing boredom.

When you have seriously considered self-image and expectations, your next job is to take practical steps towards change. Do not sit and think about it. Too much thought and introspection and too little action has been responsible for your present state of boredom. Make a list of all the things you have ever wanted to do. Be imaginative. Write down every social and leisure activity which appeals to you. Now pick out two or three which you like especially. Consider what practical steps will be necessary to start up the activities. Do you have to write or 'phone for further information? Will you have to book a place on a course or attend a club or society for specialist instruction? If possible, select some activities which can be put into effect fairly quickly and easily – for instance, joining a local club, going to further education classes, accepting an invitation to a party or holding a party of your own – and others which will take some time to get going. In this way, you will have both fairly immediate interests and longer term activities. Always have several things on the go at the same time. Remember that some interests will decline, some may not prove as attractive or stimulating as they seemed at first sight and others may not prove possible to pursue after all. By having a number of activities and interests in your life at the same time, you are not going to be dropped back suddenly to your old boring routine. Stimulating pursuits can be regarded as balloons which keep us floating above the wasteland of boredom. From time to time, these balloons burst and have to be replaced instantly to prevent us from settling back into a routine which does not provide sufficient reinforcement.

You have to take practical steps to eliminate boredom. Nobody can do it for you. Use the Antidote to control any physical and mental anxiety symptoms which you feel when planning or carrying out the stimulating pastimes. Develop Positive Self-Talk statements out of success in one area to help you sustain your interest in other activities at times of difficulty.

LIFE AREA TWO
SEXUAL ANXIETIES AND STRATEGIES

Anxiety Analysis

In order to help you find out which of the strategies in this section are likely to prove the most helpful, read through the thirty statements in the Anxiety Analysis below and note the numbers of any which are applicable to your current difficulties. Then refer to the Answer Chart, which will direct you to the appropriate strategies in this and possibly in other Life Areas as well. Where a chosen statement number appears twice then read all those strategies listed against it.

Anxiety Analysis Inventory

(1) I am anxious because I lose my erection when about to engage in sex.

(2) I become anxious when an intimate situation becomes sexual.

(3) I am anxious because I have difficulty in reaching orgasm.

(4) I am anxious because I have not experienced sexual desire for a long time.

(5) I am anxious because I masturbate.

(6) I am anxious at the thought of losing my virginity.

(7) I am anxious about my sex life now that I am approaching old age.

(8) I am anxious about being thought inexperienced by my sex partner.

(9) I am anxious because I do not think my body is attractive.

(10) I am anxious because menopause may ruin my sex life.

(11) I become anxious when I am asked to perform some sex acts with my partner.

(12) I am anxious about the size of my penis.

(13) I am anxious about the size of my breasts.
(14) I am anxious because I always seem to get into rows with my partner in circumstances which might lead to sex.
(15) I am anxious when a man makes love to me.
(16) I am anxious because I ejaculate too quickly in sexual situations.
(17) I am anxious because many of my friends swop partners.
(18) I am anxious because my partner and I consistently avoid sex.
(19) I am anxious because I do not know how to masturbate.
(20) I am anxious because I feel people will mock me since I am over sixty and I still have a strong sex drive.
(21) I am anxious because I think that starting sexual activity may hurt me physically.
(22) I become anxious when I try to discuss sex with my partner.
(23) I am anxious because I feel that I may not give my partner enough sexual satisfaction.
(24) I am anxious because I cannot achieve an erection in sexual situations.
(25) I become anxious because during intercourse my mind wanders onto non-sexual topics.
(26) I am anxious because I do not understand how female sexual arousal takes place.
(27) I am anxious because sex has become a chore rather than a pleasure.
(28) I am anxious because I feel that, at middle age, I am passing my sexual prime.
(29) I am anxious because I cannot say 'no' to unwanted sexual demands.
(30) I become anxious at the thought of sex.

Answer Chart

Statements Ticked	Most Appropriate Strategies
2, 14, 18, 22, 30	S. One (Sexual) S. One (Social) S. Four (Social) S. Five (Family) S. Nine (Family) S. Five (Work)
1, 16, 25	S. Two (Sexual)
3, 19, 15, 26	S. Three (Sexual) S. Five (Sexual) S. Nine (Family)
4, 14, 18, 23, 24, 27	S. Four (Sexual) S. Four (Social)
5, 19	S. Five (Sexual)
7, 20	S. Six (Sexual)
6, 8, 21	S. Seven (Sexual) S. Nine (Social)
10, 28	S. Eight (Sexual)
9, 12, 13	S. Nine (Sexual) S. Four (Social) S. Nine (Social) S. Five (Work)
11, 17, 29	S. Ten (Sexual) S. Two (Social) S. Nine (Family) S. Two (Work) S. Three (Work)

STRATEGY ONE

Anxiety – When Intimacy Arises

This type of anxiety arises at the point where social and mildly intimate behaviour has been replaced by an expectation or anticipation of very intimate activity. Situations where this may occur could include the end of an evening with a relatively new dating partner or even a relaxed time together with a spouse. In both cases, the anxiety level may increase markedly at the point where the circumstances of the evening change, so that sex becomes a possibility. For example, after the guests have left from a dinner party at home; after an evening out at the cinema or theatre; or after a new date has been enticed away from a party situation. So great may be the anxiety at this stage of the evening that one or both partners may at this point start an argument severe enough to produce a level of temporary ill-feeling sufficient to prevent any chance of an intimate sexual encounter. With a married couple, this may result in both partners adopting a 'back to back' position in bed, each thinking, as they drift off to sleep: 'Well, if he/she is going to behave like that, I'm certainly not going to do anything about it.'

This type of row can be seen as an *avoidance response* which obviates the possibility of sex and therefore removes the anxiety. As I explained in Part One, this type of *negative reinforcement*, that is the removal of an unpleasant or distressing situation, helps to establish the avoidance response. It becomes increasingly likely that the couple will adopt the strategy of 'having a row' whenever sexual tension rises and that these rows may encroach earlier and earlier into a social evening. The couple who constantly bicker across the dinner table, shout at one another during a cocktail party and row over the details of their trip to the theatre may well be establishing the 'reasons' why they will not be able to have sex together later that night.

Rows, although a common method of escape from the anxiety produced by the thought of sex, are not the only methods by which intimate situations can be defused. A second popular avoidance tactic in certain social groups might be termed the *Hampstead Syndrome*, since it involves a studious intellectualisation of the feelings and meanings behind sexuality – a guaranteed method of turning yourself off sex! It works like this. As the sexual situation develops a couple who want to use the intellectual way out will start to discuss, with great seriousness, such subjects as 'optimal sexual frequency'; 'desirable duration of intercourse' or the 'need for variety'. All of which are usually destined to result in no sexual intercourse at all.

There are a number of stages which have to be gone through by a couple as their relationship changes from first acquaintance to sexual intimacy. This may take from several weeks to several minutes depending on the personalities and circumstances. The stages include the initial conversation, the making of dates, touching and intimate conversation, intimate environments, petting and finally sexual intercourse. A person who experiences anxiety in situations which lead to sex may function perfectly well during the early stages. The man will find himself able to sustain a strong erection when clothed and the woman may be lubricated and aroused in the same situation. But when the final barrier to sex, the removal of clothes, has been overcome, the anxiety can rise to such a level that it interferes drastically with sexual arousal.

Strategies

In Part One, I explained that the anxiety response is generated by the *sympathetic* branch of the *autonomic nervous system*. Sexual arousal, on the other hand, is a *parasympathetic* response. Since these two branches work in *opposition* to one another, it is clear that a high level of *sympathetic* arousal, that is great anxiety, will effectively prevent sexual arousal, that is erection in the male, lubrication in the female and the inability to reach or control orgasm. These will be discussed in more detail in Strategies Two and Three.

As explained earlier, the *autonomic nervous system* is not under the direct control of the 'thinking' part of the brain, so no amount of 'positive thinking' or exhortation will help you conquer this, or indeed any other, type of anxiety response.

The starting point for overcoming this type of anxiety is to be on the lookout for any form of avoidance behaviour, such as rows which grow out of nothing in particular, that has the effect of preventing social intimacy from developing into a mutually desired sexual intimacy. Once you realise the real reason for such arguments or excuses, which stem from anxiety rather than from any deepfelt desire by either partner to avoid sex, it should be much easier to eliminate them. But remember that if this type of behaviour has been established over a long period of time, patience and the co-operation of both partners will be needed to remove it.

The best method of doing this is to reduce the anxieties associated with sexual intimacy by *self-disclosure* of personal difficulties or hang-ups. Such disclosure is often very difficult at first, especially for the man. The propaganda of many male-orientated magazines has led to a completely artificial concept of sexual athleticism. This has made it much harder for some men to admit to any sexual anxieties or problems at all. They strive to achieve what they believe to be the male 'sexual norm' and become extremely anxious if anything goes 'wrong'. Both sexes may be inhibited about talking frankly and honestly about their sexual problems and needs, even to partners with whom they have lived for many years. Such inhibitions may stem from early training that sex was not a proper subject for serious discussion or it may arise out of a fear that any confession of weakness will be used as ammunition at a later time.

In any self-disclosure interchange, somebody has to make the first move. If you would like to talk about certain anxiety difficulties with your partner but are uncertain of his or her response, I suggest that you ask them to read this strategy and, if they have any views on the matter, to make them known to you. In this way, you may be able to start a general debate on sexual anxieties in general which can gradually be led into a discussion of your own particular difficulties. You may also find it helpful to read further strategies in this section, especially Two; Three; Six; Eight; Nine and Ten, which deal with specific problems.

STRATEGY TWO

Anxieties – When Erection Difficulties Occur

Premature ejaculation and the inability to sustain an erection are two commonly occurring male sexual difficulties which generate, and are caused by high levels of anxiety. Except in the rare instances of physiological impairment, such as neurological lesions or the subsidiary effects of diabetes, these problems can be directly attributed to the effects of the *sympathetic* nervous system. The basis of this problem is that sexual arousal, as opposed to orgasm with its associated ejaculation and loss of erection, is a *parasympathetic* response. Orgasm, being a *sympathetic* response, may result too quickly or erection may be lost if a person enters a sexual situation whilst physically or mentally anxious.

Strategies

The way to overcome these difficulties is to maintain as deep a level of *parasympathetic* arousal as possible during sex. The first strategy which might be used is to carry out Quick Relaxation at frequent intervals during foreplay and coitus in order to bring the mechanical aspects of sex under your direct control. This can best be carried out with the knowledge and co-operation of your partner following self-disclosure of your difficulties. (See Strategy One.) Men with this type of problem very often try to 'force' themselves to maintain an erection or prevent premature ejaculation, a strategy which usually results in the situation getting worse. If you slow down or take occasional pauses, during which stimulation of the penis ceases, this may, in the majority of cases, overcome the difficulty.

If this does not remove the problem, you may need to start

earlier and use a more basic approach such as I describe in Strategy Four.

Another cause of this problem may be that a position is adopted during intercourse which is more consistent with a *sympathetic* than a *parasympathetic* response. For example, the comparatively more strenuous face-to-face position, where the man with difficulties is on top of his partner, may produce a much greater level of physical tension than a position where he is lying on his back with his partner on top of him in a squatting position. In this latter position, the man may be able to relax his body much more effectively while his partner can move up and down on his penis. Another position which, for most people, is less strenuous than the face-to-face 'missionary position', is the rear entry into the vagina, where both partners are either kneeling or lying on their sides one behind the other. With both these methods of entry, the man neither has to deal with weight on his own body nor support himself in a strenuous position. Success in these sexual positions can produce increasing confidence and more strenuous positions can gradually be introduced. I would emphasise that the co-operation of the partner is of the utmost importance, especially at those times when a rest pause is needed. This can only be satisfactorily obtained through a frank self-disclosure of the difficulties being experienced, as suggested and described in Strategy One in this section.

A third cause of the difficulty may be an attempt to delay orgasm by the frequently adopted method of turning thoughts onto non-sexual topics, for example, counting or thinking about work. This is usually doubly inefficient as it not only produces mental stress, which can increase the level of anxiety and so make the problem worse, but it also removes the pleasure of intercourse itself. A much more effective method, which avoids both these dangers, is to focus attention on the sensations of love-making themselves and take rest pauses when necessary. In Strategy Three, I describe the concept of passive concentration which involves a relaxed acceptance of the physical and mental pleasures of intercourse. There should be no forcing of the pace and no pessimistic thoughts of failure. The feelings should be allowed to wash over you without making any attempt to analyse or comment on them. In this way, the rest pauses become highly arousing and enjoyable as well as being the most effective means of delaying orgasm or maintaining an erection. It sometimes requires practice to achieve this state of passive concentration but, so long as you have an understanding, sensitive and co-operative partner, the practice sessions should be both enjoyable and sexually satisfactory. In the absence of such co-operation, a man can practise during masturbation. (See Strategy Five.)

A method which has been popularised for dealing with premature ejaculation difficulties is the so-called 'Squeeze' technique. Because it is widely discussed in sex therapy manuals, it is referred to here even though clinical experience shows that the rest pause method is generally more effective and much less troublesome. In the Squeeze technique, the man tells his partner when he is about to reach the point of ejaculation and his partner then squeezes the end of his erect penis by placing a thumb against the frenulum or underside of the penis (the area where the tip of the penis or glans joins the shaft on the underside) and the two first fingers on the corona (the ridge which marks the boundary between the tip of the penis and the shaft on the upper side) and squeezes firmly for about ten seconds. The effect of this is to reduce the man's sexual arousal and to remove the desire to ejaculate. The penis often goes slightly soft following the squeeze and you can then go on to rearouse it by stimulating it as before. When used in coitus, the man must obviously withdraw his penis for his partner to apply the squeeze.

STRATEGY THREE

Anxieties – When Trying to Achieve Orgasm

This problem is usually a combination of physical anxiety or stimulation difficulties, too much effort and a prediction of failure. Female sexual arousal is predominantly a *parasympathetic* state, which means that for it to be carried out effectively the woman should be both mentally and physically relaxed. Excessive anxiety about the sex act, inappropriate stimulation which may lead to irritation or excessive demand on herself to reach orgasm are likely to produce *sympathetic* or anxiety responses when she needs to be in a *parasympathetic* or relaxed state.

The orgasm itself is a *sympathetic* response in which heightened respiration, increased heart rate and sweating are the most obvious characteristics. However, this *sympathetic* state should be reached via an adequate period of *parasympathetic* arousal to get to a point where the woman can let go and allow orgasm to take over.

Strategies

The crucial stages in achieving female orgasm are as follows. First, the woman must be in an anxiety-free state in order that she may become sexually aroused either by herself or by her partner. This means being able, when necessary, to relax for a few seconds or minutes in order to allow any anxiety which may have developed to be overcome. Quick Relaxation methods may be used here and will be especially effective if some light, non-sexual massage is given by her partner or by herself at the same time.

Secondly, she should learn to appreciate any stimulation through a process of *passive concentration*. By this, I mean that instead of either trying to force an orgasm to occur or assuming a pessimistic attitude about the chances of achieving orgasm, the woman should simply accept and allow herself to be enveloped by the sensations arising from sexual stimulation. In other words, rather than striving to attain a certain level of arousal, she should *allow* the level of arousal to build up by concentrating on it when it has already occurred. Achieving this change of attitude is often very difficult for a woman who has been concerned about her orgasm for some time. She may have to practise on a number of occasions in order to appreciate and recognise the beneficial effects of such a passive approach. The necessary practice can be carried out either on her own or with a co-operative partner. This will require discussion of the problem and self-disclosure of the type described in Strategy One. If such self-disclosure proves difficult or the required co-operation is not forthcoming, then masturbation techniques will prove extremely effective. Since a woman knows her own body far better than any man is likely to, she can decide very quickly how she wants any stimulation to be varied.

The third stage concerns the type of stimulating itself. There is now little doubt, following extensive research investigations such as Masters and Johnson and the personal disclosures of many female writers on the topic, that the focus of stimulation of the attainment of orgasm in the female is the clitoris as opposed to the vagina. Equally it is now clear that individual women appreciate clitoral stimulation in different ways and in different combinations with the stimulation of other parts of their bodies. Whether the overall stimulation includes the lips, the breasts, the anus, the stomach, the buttocks or the vagina (with fingers or the penis) the central component in the arousal is clitoral stimulation.

The clitoris is a small protuberance situated where the smaller inner lips of the vagina meet and are found by drawing the fingers gently up from the vaginal opening towards the pubic hair for between one and two centimetres. It becomes distinctly erect when sexual arousal takes place as the whole area of the vulva, that is the external area of the female genitals, becomes engorged with blood and reddens deeply.

There are several ways in which the clitoris can be stimulated during the sexual act. For example, during coitus the man may provide clitoral stimulation by thrusting deeply into the vagina so that his pubic bone rubs consistently against the clitoris; the woman can slide her hand down to her pubic area so that she can massage the clitoris with her fingers; or the man can massage the clitoris with his fingers while his penis is in the vagina.

Alternatively, before or after coitus the man can use his fingers to caress the clitoris, his tongue to lick the clitoral area or his lips to suck gently on the clitoris while his tongue caresses it.

Before leaving this important subject, we should point out that many women who have previously not achieved orgasm have done so when they applied a vibrator to the clitoral area. There is some evidence to indicate that this mechanical way of arriving at orgasm is based on the rate of vibration of the clitoris and its nerve endings and is likely to work very quickly whatever the mental state of the woman concerned. The vibrator can be used alone or with the partner and with or without coitus being involved.

The fourth and final stage in female orgasm is probably the most crucial and certainly the least discussed. This is how to let go from the *parasympathetic* state of being gradually more and more aroused and *allowing* the body to switch into the *sympathetic* state of orgasm. Notice that in describing this particular stage we used the word 'allow'. This, rather than any attempt at forcing the body towards climax, is the key to achieving orgasm. It is at this point of maximal arousal that many women find a difficulty in allowing themselves to let go, sometimes because they are afraid of losing control in general and sometimes because the stimulation is either insufficient or too intense. The strategy for achieving this stage of release is once again *passive concentration* where the mounting levels of arousal are allowed to flood over the woman without being forced or in any way being evaluated other than to feel that they are enjoyable. At the point where the woman feels that she is about to spill over into a state of orgasm, she may wish the man to slow up and become more sensitive with his stimulation. In this case she should indicate these needs by guiding his hands or mouth or rate of thrusting. It is also often quite helpful for her to bring on the *sympathetic* components of orgasm, that is increased respiration, muscular tension and rapid heart rate, by deliberately breathing deeply and holding the breath in for a period and often by tensing the muscles, just at the point when she feels she must let go. This will often trigger off the other components of orgasm which then occurs fully. What often happens at the moment when she should let go is that the woman suddenly gives up, relaxes abruptly, shakes her head and says: 'No, no, no, I can't make it . . .' and so loses the momentum needed to peak into orgasm.

It is emphasised that you may need to practise this *passive concentration* approach to the final stage of orgasm and might need several sessions of building up to the peak, quite possibly within the same act, before you finally allow yourself to let go.

STRATEGY FOUR

Anxieties – When Sexual Activity Ceases

When sexual activity between a couple has ceased or in cases where an individual has withdrawn from sexual interactions, there is usually a history of a slow decline associated with high levels of anxiety. It is only in fairly rare cases that there is an abrupt cessation of all sexual behaviour. Most frequently it can be seen as a gradually established *avoidance response* which is *negatively reinforced* (as described in Part One) by the removal of distressing anxiety symptoms.

The anxieties which produce this type of gradual withdrawal from, and the subsequent avoidance of, sexual activity are often based on a concern about performance. The anxious person will spend a great deal of time before, after and even during sexual intercourse wondering if they are giving satisfaction. They will try to put themselves into the mind of their partner, and view their performance in a negative and highly critical way employing such 'double think' attitudes as: 'I wonder what she thinks about my virility?' 'I wonder if he thinks I am really getting sufficient enjoyment?' 'I wonder if he/she thinks badly of me for my poor performance?'

Frequently, the focus of these anxieties will be one particular aspect of the sex act, usually coital proficiency: 'Will I get an erection?' 'Will I sustain an erection?' 'Will I achieve an orgasm?'

By concentrating exclusively on this 'problem' aspect of intercourse, a bogey is set up which effectively prevents the partners from considering other equally pleasurable and important aspects of the sex act. In many cases, the sub-goals of sexual behaviour, which are necessary to achieve the 'problem' goal, will have been either forgotten or have come to be regarded as unimportant. For example, a man suffering from premature ejaculation difficulties or a woman who has been unable to achieve a desired orgasm on a number of occasions, may concentrate entirely on reaching these coital goals. The sub-goals of relaxed intimacy leading to sexually arousing foreplay, with the components of caressing, massaging, fondling and similar forms of stimulation, may have become brief and perfunctory in the extreme as both partners hurry towards their area of sexual concern. The whole interaction has then become a negative spiral, in which more and more attention is concentrated on the single piece of problem behaviour, while less and less time is given to the essential stepping stones by which it can be reached. If you have withdrawn from sexual activity because of this type of anxiety, a basic restructuring of your whole approach to sex may be necessary. If there is some other reason for your having ceased to have sexual intercourse, even though you still desire to do so, you may find guidance in Strategies One, Six, Seven, Eight, Nine and Ten in this section.

Strategies

In order to break the negative spiral and re-create a positive one, it is usually necessary to take the quite drastic step of stopping any attempt at attaining the *bogey* goal which has become over-important and to concentrate exclusively on the neglected sub-goals.

This can best be done by establishing a programme in which, over a number of love-making sessions, you work with your partner on a series of pleasure-giving exercises which gradually increase in demandingness and complexity.

Start by deciding on a period each day when you will be relaxed and can spend about half an hour together. For the first few days, occupy this time by taking off all your clothes and in turn massaging and stroking each other's body in a non-sexual way. Concentrate on parts of the body which are not directly associated with sexual arousal, especially, of course, avoiding the genital area. Learn what type of caressing your partner needs and likes. By taking it in turns we mean that one of you should start by being the giver in the situation while the other partner simply lies there and receives the sensation without having to do anything in return. After a few minutes, the situation is reversed so that both partners have acted as givers and receivers in turn. When you are *receiving* the massage, try to guide your partner's stimulations through hands and mouth in as explicit a way as you can. Tell him or her what you would like to have done, where you enjoyed being massaged and the pressure and pace of the stroking. Remember to confine such massage to the back, chest, buttocks, legs, neck, face and head for the first few sessions. It is often useful to apply a massaging oil or talcum powder to your partner's body when carrying out this exercise. When you have become relaxed and confident in this stage, you should build up on it by including stimulation, in a non-demanding way, of the genital area. Use this opportunity to explore your partner's genital areas thoroughly and to discover how he or she responds to various types of stimulation. Use different parts of your body, such as fingers, lips, tongue or even breasts to massage and stimulate. But at this stage do not attempt to force the issue of obvious sexual arousal or orgasm and avoid genital to genital contact.

When you are comfortable with this stage then go on, armed with the information which you have gathered about how your partner likes to be stimulated, to carry out more prolonged and vigorous stimulation to assist sexual arousal and orgasm. At first, try this without genital/genital contact and only when you are quite comfortable begin to introduce genital/genital contact.

Once you have achieved coitus and overcome the bogey which had become the focus of sexual anxieties, you should not neglect the earlier stages of the programme. These sub-goals can become very pleasurable activities in their own right and by frequently exercising them you will be able to enjoy a more varied and sensual sex life.

STRATEGY FIVE

Anxieties – When Masturbating

Many people, especially teenagers, experience high levels of guilt-induced anxiety when they masturbate. This can be seen largely as a legacy of the attitudes of religion and certain prejudiced sections of nineteenth-century medical opinion. It may seem extraordinary to some people that such views should persist into the latter part of the twentieth century but clinical experience and the published findings of sexologists in Europe and America clearly show that this is in fact the case.

Strategies

Let me start by saying quite firmly that masturbation is actually *beneficial* to your health. It does not harm you in any way, or weaken you sexually. Indeed, I would suggest that the most appropriate strategy for those anxious about masturbation is that they learn how to do it effectively and enjoyably. Let us begin by considering male masturbation. The most commonly employed masturbation techniques for men include grasping the shaft of the penis, the skin of which is rubbed backwards and forwards, with or without the simultaneous stimulation of the tip or glans of the penis, either with the other hand or by moving the foreskin backwards and forwards over it. This is continued until ejaculation and orgasm are achieved. This technique is often assisted by the use of a lubricant such as KY jelly or baby oil. Another method involves the man's lying face down on a bed or similar surface and simulating the act of coitus by rubbing his erect penis against the surface on which he is lying. During this time, the physical act is usually accompanied by a fantasy of sexual activities with other people. Such fantasies are quite normal and can also be considered beneficial. Be uninhibited in your fantasy life and use it as a practice session when you can think of sensual activities to carry out with a partner. Masturbation can also be used by the man to learn how to extend his period of sensuality before ejaculation (see Strategy Two). This can be done by 'teasing' the penis so that the arousal is built up to a point just prior to ejaculation and then a rest pause enjoyed. In this way, men can often learn to have a series of mini-orgasms by a process of 'sexual brinkmanship' before eventually ejaculating.

Female masturbation is usually achieved by stimulation of the clitoris (see Strategy Three) by the fingers, palm of hand or an object such as a vibrator, hairbrush handle, or even a soft toy. The stimulation is carried out by a consistent rubbing of the clitoris which may, at the very beginning, be lubricated by a spot of KY jelly but which will later be lubricated by natural vaginal secretions. Again, the woman can learn to tease herself by resting just before orgasm occurs and so having a series of small pleasure peaks before finally reaching orgasm. If there is any difficulty in beginning masturbation, it is often helpful to carry out an exploration of the genital area by looking at the vulva (the external parts of the genitals) with a mirror or by starting to masturbate in a naturally sensual environment such as lying in a warm bath and soaping yourself. This latter technique means also that you will start off in a relaxed *parasympathetic* state, induced by the warmth of the bath.

STRATEGY SIX

Anxieties – When Sex Declines with Ageing

This anxiety may in part be due to a mixture of actual decline in sexual need and sexual pursuit, brought about by hormonal changes associated with ageing. But of equal importance is the *expectation* that sexual appetite will decrease with age. This psychological factor often exaggerates the actual physical changes of age, which themselves may not be very pronounced, to such an extent that sexual activity may cease.

Strategies

The first essential is to reject the attitude that ageing *inevitably* means the decline or cessation of sexual appetite or ability. Ageism, the idea prevalent in Western society that there are certain things which people beyond a certain age cannot decently do, should be totally rejected. Chronological ageing ought to be seen for what it is, little more than a bureaucratic convenience which serves to trigger off various functions of the State machinery, determining for example those allowed to vote, marry without parental consent, retire from work or receive certain financial benefits. Any kind of prejudice based on the fact that a person is at a particular chronological age has no credibility in fact. Yet the image of the 'dirty old man' is a powerful and all-pervading one which makes many men and women over the age of, say, sixty, feel that they are behaving perversely if they not only seek sexual activities but have the temerity actually to enjoy them. Do not let yourself be persuaded by this type of propaganda into believing that what you are doing or want to do sexually is in any way wrong.

Having liberated yourself from these artificially imposed constraints, you should then look to your general health. Sexual function, like any other piece of the body's machinery, depends to a great extent on the health of the overall structure. If you have not taken much exercise, you should start on a programme of mild fitness training. Check with your doctor if you have any heart or respiration problems and he or she will advise you on the level of activities which you can safely undertake. Swimming, brisk walking or jogging not only build stamina but also make you look slimmer and trimmer. Watch your diet. Many people in later life tend to neglect their nutrition, either by eating too much in relation to the amount of energy-burning activity they undertake, or poorly so far as the balance of protein, carbohydrate and vitamin intake is concerned. Eat a mixed diet which includes protein (meat, fish, etc) and fresh fruit and vegetables. Avoid high carbohydrate foodstuffs, especially those which contain a great deal of sugar.

By taking exercise and eating sensibly, you should not only help yourself to feel fitter but you will also look healthier and more attractive as you shed excess pounds.

Appearance is important not only for your self-confidence but to make you look attractive to your sexual partner. Here again, social prejudice based on ageism tends to mock the efforts of people, after a certain age, to look good. 'Mutton dressed up as lamb' is a phrase often used to ridicule a man or woman in later life who has made an effort to look their best.

Continue to think about sex and enjoy regular sexual activity either alone or with a partner. Do not be ashamed of your sexual desires and needs.

STRATEGY SEVEN

Anxieties – When Virginity is Lost

This anxiety is often based either on a physical fear that the loss of virginity may be painful or uncomfortable, or on a worry that the partner may be disappointed because of an inevitable lack of experience.

Strategies

Both types of anxiety can be overcome by disclosing them to the partner and asking to be helped over the process of losing virginity by taking it slowly and sensuously so that it is a good experience to remember rather than a difficult one to forget.

So far as men are concerned, the chief worry is usually one of appearing clumsy and inexperienced when having sex with a more sophisticated partner, whether a female or a male. With some male homosexuals there is also a fear that anal intercourse, which is often regarded by homosexuals without practical experience as the only form of homosexual behaviour, will be painful. It is true that anal penetration, whether in a homosexual or heterosexual interaction, is an experience which many confess to having found uncomfortable on the first few occasions. The anal sphincter muscles need to be trained to accept a penis but once this has been achieved any initial discomfort should cease. If you are an inexperienced homosexual, you should not assume that anal penetration is the only type of sexual activity possible. Research and clinical experience has shown that many homosexuals prefer oral sex or mutual stimulation using the hands to anal penetration.

Muscular tension brought about by anxieties over the loss of virginity can make both vaginal and anal penetration much more difficult for the active partner and far less pleasurable for the passive partner. A slow process of arousal brought about by sensitive and sensual foreplay will ensure that the bodies of both partners are in a *parasympathetic*, that is, a very relaxed, state before penetration takes place.

If you are going to lose your virginity to an experienced partner then self-disclose your concern about whether it will be satisfactory. Admit your virginity and allow the experienced partner to guide and teach you. Far from being contemptuous, the experienced partner is most likely to be excited and rather honoured to help you learn about sexual behaviour from them. It could be argued that one of the best ways for a young man to learn about sex is from an older and more mature partner. If your partner is no more experienced than you are, then enjoy your mutual explorations and learning. Do not rush towards any idealised goals which you may have derived from popular magazines or cinema concepts of physical love. Share and take pleasure from both your successes and your set-backs when exploring each other's needs and responses.

For the girl, the loss of virginity means that her vaginal canal will have to learn how to accommodate a penis and the hymen (if still intact) must be broken. The hymen is a thin membrane of skin located just inside the vaginal opening and stretched across the vagina so as to partially cover it. The hymen is often torn before actual intercourse in girls who have used internal sanitary tampons during their periods, engaged in physically exerting exercise or inserted objects into their vagina during masturbation.

It is important to understand that the vagina is capable of accommodating a wide range of penis sizes quite comfortably as long as it is well lubricated. It is most important that early experiences of intercourse should occur after a good deal of sexual arousal and lubrication have been achieved. Any pain or discomfort experienced through the rupturing of the hymen during intercourse will be very short in duration and will quickly be forgotten in the pleasures of the sex act which has come at the end of a period of sexual foreplay.

STRATEGY EIGHT

Anxieties – When Going through the Menopause

Anxiety over sexual functioning during and after menopause is due mainly to cultural expectations and predictions. In some instances, there may be temporary disturbances in sexual function which may generate concern that the woman's sex life has reached an end.

Strategies

It is important to understand that the hormonal changes which occur during menopause in no way mean that sexual activity becomes any less pleasurable or possible than during the years preceding the so-called 'change of life'. In fact, many women experience a marked increase in their frequency and enjoyment of intercourse after menopause and often attribute this to the fact that they can now enjoy sex without any fears of unwanted pregnancies. The actual period of the change may well produce uncomfortable side effects which can mean that sexual activity suffers because of an overall decline in general performance. However, during the period of change you should try not to allow sexual activity to disappear completely but rather to keep it ticking over gently by maintaining sensual contact with your partner until, after you have passed through the change, you can begin to settle back into a regular sex life again. Many women, of course, pass through menopause without any difficulties at all and you should not assume that you will meet any of the problems which you may have heard or read about.

The concept of the male menopause has recently been popularised and it does seem that some men experience, at a psychological level, disturbances similar to those encountered by women. Once again it is important, if there is any sexual decline, for such behaviour not to be allowed to disappear completely. It is often all to easy to adopt a policy of expedience and allow sexual activity to disappear through apathy or indifference, at this time. Remember that it is much easier to *increase* a low rate of sexual behaviour than it is to restart a piece of behaviour which has for a time completely disappeared.

STRATEGY NINE

Anxieties – When Considering Physical Appearance

Anxieties about genital size and physical appearance are widespread and cause a great deal of distress especially amongst adolescents whose bodies are in a state of rapid change. Negative thoughts about supposed inadequacies can lead to the avoidance of such situations as dating, going to social gatherings, petting or sexual intercourse. The frustrations which this avoidance produces can lead to the person developing a hatred of their bodies. This in turn is likely to undermine their self-confidence and subsequent social and sexual performance.

Strategies

Do not allow commercial pressure from advertisements, romantic fiction and the cinema delude you into believing that there is any such thing as a physical ideal. The chemistry of mutual attraction and what elements in one person's appearance make them seem desirable or sexually exciting to another, are often unfathomable to those outside the relationship. Some women prefer a slim, flat-bellied male in their lives – others are only attracted by a large chested, heavily built man. Some men prefer girls with large breasts, while others are only turned on by slim boyish figures.

Perhaps these comments seem self-evident. To many people they will be. Yet the amount of unhappiness and anxiety generated by a refusal to accept the varied nature of appearance and attraction is terrifying. Teenagers of both sexes agonise over their looks, physique and complexion. Some come close to suicide because they refuse even to consider that anybody could ever find them desirable.

If you are in this position, you must rest assured that, however negative you may currently feel about your own body, there will be people who find it attractive and desirable.

It is important for your self-confidence, health and social prospects, that you learn to love your body. Seek out and admire those parts which you consider attractive, perhaps your eyes or smile, your hair or hands. If there are things which you dislike but which can be changed, by make-up, a different hair style or any other form of simple beauty treatment, then make these changes. Do not consider it wrong to want to pamper your body and look your best. Those parts which you dislike but cannot change, you must learn to love with the rest. They are part of your uniqueness as a human being – a statement of your individuality. Avoid making negative statements about yourself, either mentally or to your friends. They are probably not true or if true they are most likely exaggerated. Even if they are objectively correct they are unlikely to be improved by the kind of destructive soul-searching many people indulge in. The only way in which you will determine whether your body is pleasing to someone is by making a relationship with them and experiencing their responses. It is inevitable that you will experience some rejections and probably also be responsible for rejecting the advances of some others. But if you *never* make the attempt to socialise because of anxieties about your body you may always believe that your small breasts, or thin legs, a hairy chest or buck teeth would have precluded you from making successful relationships (see Strategy Nine (Social)).

Penis size is frequently a source of concern to a man, almost always because they feel that it is undersized. In the flaccid state there is considerable variation in size but this tends to even out when the penis becomes erect. The average size of the penis is five and a half inches, which is much shorter than most men believe. But lengths greater or smaller than this can easily be accommodated by the very flexible vagina. Bear in mind that other men's organs always look larger than your own because the angle at which you usually look at your own penis tends to foreshorten it.

STRATEGY TEN

Anxieties – When Confronted with Sexual Variations

This anxiety arises out of different sexual preferences between the two partners. Your partner may require oral sex or want to act out fantasies while you prefer more conventional penile/vaginal coitus. Your partner may be pressing for partner swapping or group sex while you find such ideas repulsive. A prime cause of anxiety here is often the demands by one partner that the other changes to suit their tastes. A refusal to do so may, it is feared, lead to a break in the relationship.

Strategies

In this sort of situation it is important to retain your own right to refuse to take part in any activity which you feel disinclined to experience. There may, however, be some activities which you would like to try out but are afraid to experiment with, because you feel that your partner may rush you or make excessive demands. For this reason you should first explain to your partner that you would like to explore the possibilities, but reserve the right to withdraw if you decide that it is not for you. Do not feel that, having embarked experimentally on exploring an area about which you are unsure, you cannot back out even if you have gone in some way already. It is never too late to change your mind no matter what the other participants in the situation may say. It will be much easier for you to deal with any unkind comments because you have decided not to continue, than to handle any possible self-recriminations because you were too weak to refuse. Ultimately, in any sexual act, you should only do what you wish to do. But your right to say 'no' must always be balanced by the self-evident fact that unless you experience a particular piece of behaviour you will never know whether or not it is for you.

In declining your partner's requests you should always act in an assertive rather than an aggressive manner. Do not try to conceal your own anxieties over the piece of behaviour behind a smoke screen of ridicule and abuse of your partner.

LIFE AREA THREE
FAMILY AND CHILD RELATED ANXIETIES AND STRATEGIES

Anxiety Analysis

In order to help you find out which of the strategies in this section are likely to prove the most helpful, read through the thirty statements in the Anxiety Analysis below and note the numbers of any which are applicable to your current difficulties. Then refer to the Answer Chart which will direct you to the appropriate strategies in this and possibly in other Life Areas as well.

Anxiety Analysis Inventory

(1) I am anxious because my child seems so unhappy at school.
(2) I am anxious because I cannot express my point-of-view to my partner.
(3) I am anxious when I have to go out of the house.
(4) I am anxious because my child plays truant from school.
(5) I am anxious because my partner is so dependent on me.
(6) I am anxious because my partner never wants to talk to me when he/she comes home in the evening.
(7) I am anxious because my child cries excessively.
(8) I am anxious because my child refuses to go to school.
(9) I am anxious because my partner refuses to take his/her share of the family responsibilities.
(10) I am anxious because my child has a fantasy friend.
(11) I am anxious because my child has temper tantrums.
(12) I am anxious because I cannot seem to demonstrate emotions to my partner.

(13) I am anxious because I have to take all the decisions at home.

(14) I am anxious when I fly on holiday with my family.

(15) I am anxious because my child wets the bed.

(16) I am anxious when I have to take the children to school.

(17) I am anxious because I cannot tell my partner how much I love him/her.

(18) I am anxious because my children are going to leave home.

(19) I am anxious because I know my children will make mistakes once they leave home.

(20) I am anxious because I cannot assert myself with my partner.

(21) I am anxious because I cannot hold a conversation with my partner.

(22) I am anxious when I am criticised by my partner.

(23) I am anxious because my partner and I cannot seem to agree on things.

(24) I am anxious because my child refuses to eat certain foods or has a fad.

(25) I am anxious because my child does not seem to make friends.

(26) I am anxious because my child is so miserable at starting school.

(27) I become anxious when I feel angry towards my partner.

(28) I become anxious because my partner always wants me to make the first sexual advance.

(29) I am anxious because I cannot get time to myself at home.

(30) I am anxious because of the demands made on me by my family.

Answer Chart

Statements Ticked	Most Appropriate Strategies
7, 11	S. One (Family)
1, 4, 8, 16, 25, 26	S. Two (Family) S. Five (Social)
10, 24	S. Three (Family)
15	S. Four (Family)
2, 6, 20, 21, 22, 23, 29	S. Five (Family) S. One (Social) S. Two (Social) S. Four (Social) S. One (Sexual) S. Ten (Sexual) S. Three (Work) S. Five (Work) S. Nine (Work)
3, 16	S. Six (Family)
5, 9, 13, 28, 30	S. Seven (Family) S. Seven (Social) S. Four (Sexual)
14	S. Eight (Family) S. Five (Social)
18, 19	S. Ten (Family)
12, 17, 27	S. Nine (Family) S. Six (Social) S. One (Sexual) S. Two (Work) S. Three (Work)

STRATEGY ONE

Anxieties – When the Baby Cries

Most mothers will claim that they can tell the difference between crying in response to real pain or discomfort and crying which is due to boredom or lack of attention. There are no rules on this, but it would appear from mothers' reports that the first sort of crying is sharper and more urgent whereas the second sort of crying has more the quality of whimpering and whining. Obviously, the urgent cry for help of a child in distress is one which a parent must attend to quickly and consistently. But the cry of a child who has woken up briefly in the night and become a little bored, who refuses to be put down to sleep at night or is just generally whining during the day, is one which can safely be brought under control. Included with this type of crying is the temper tantrum, or aggressive outburst, of some young children. These types of behaviour are almost always attention seeking and if they are consistently rewarded with that attention, they will increase in frequency as the behaviour is *positively reinforced*. It is also worth pointing out something which you may have gathered from our discussion of learning and the role of reinforcement in Part One. As the child is being *positively reinforced* by attention – even a scolding or punishing attention can be a form of positive reinforcement – the mother is being *negatively reinforced* for giving that attention by the removal of the unpleasant behaviour on the part of the child. This means that 'crying behaviour to demand attention' and 'attending behaviour to remove the irritant' can quickly become established patterns.

Strategies

The most appropriate method of dealing with this problem is to break the pattern of mutual reinforcement by withdrawing attention when the crying or temper tantrum behaviour occurs. At the same time, however, since this type of behaviour is a general indication that attention may be low, steps should be taken to increase the overall level of attention at times when the child is behaving appropriately. Reward and reinforce the child with your interest and involvement at times when he or she is playing happily or carrying out some absorbing hobby so that this behaviour, rather than the crying or tantrums, becomes more and more frequent. What is being advocated here is not the removal of all attention from an already possibly impoverished situation but, rather, the reassigning and increasing of attention at more appropriate times.

There are two main difficulties in using this strategy. Firstly, you may find it hard *not* to give the child immediate attention. Remember that this response on your part has probably been *negatively reinforced* over a period of many months or even years. If you stop giving attention, you may feel guilty of neglect or anxious that there really is something the matter. Even if the behaviour is clearly attention seeking, you may still feel unjustified in ignoring it. Bear in mind, however, that your child will actually be receiving increasing attention from you as the crying and/or temper tantrums diminish and they become more interesting and agreeable to be with. These *positive reinforcers* will help to establish the new response on your part.

The second difficulty is that in the early days of implementing this strategy there will almost certainly be a marked *increase* in attention seeking behaviour. The outbursts are likely to become more frequent, louder and more prolonged. *Do not worry.* This is only to be expected. The child is simply trying to win back the old rewards of attention by stepping up behaviours which were previously very successful in obtaining them. You must stand your ground, however difficult the first week or so proves.

If you give in half way through, the disruptive behaviour is likely to become worse. Continue with the strategy until behavioural change occurs. Be quick to reinforce the new and desirable responses. You will probably find it easier to handle this strategy if you wait until you are well advanced in your own Antidote training.

STRATEGY TWO

Anxieties – When Children Start School

For most children, going to school for the first time is the first major change in their lifestyle. It is hardly surprising that some of them find it hard to cope with the drastic change in their routine or to make the necessary adjustments without anxiety. Once at school, the child can encounter problems in relating to school friends; difficulties with academic work; and distressing interactions with teachers. All of these can give rise to anxieties about going to school. The worry the child feels about going to school can also, in some cases, be due to anxiety about leaving the parental home in case something goes wrong there. All of these potential sources of anxiety have to be taken into account when considering how to help the child who has difficulties in going to school.

Strategies

1. Beginning School

Anxieties here can be greatly reduced by some simple preparation in the few days prior to starting school. First, ensure that the child is familiar with his or her new school by taking them to look around and meet some of the staff. Secondly, see that the child has most of the basic skills necessary to fit into the school's routine. They should be taught how to address the teachers so that they do not become unduly reticent in the classroom. They should also know how to play a number of infant games so that they are not left out of things during breaks. If they have brothers or sisters of the same age, they will probably have learned how to interact effectively with other infants. But the only child, or a child whose brothers and sisters are a great deal older, may never have fully developed this ability. Remember that making new friends and developing relationships with others is a learned skill which will only be done well as a result of constant practice. You should encourage your child to make as many friends of his or her own age as possible. If for any reason this cannot be done, you should consider arranging training sessions during which you role-play the part of another child. Do not simply tell your child how games, sports and other infant school activities are carried out. Show them. Play with them in order for them to learn how to play. This may sound like common sense and probably most parents do provide their child with these initial social skills. Yet, in many cases where the child has a high level of anxiety when starting school, the basic difficulty turns out to be a lack of simple social skills. You must never assume, as some parents seem to, that these will arise spontaneously. These skills must be constantly practised if they are to become 'natural' and 'spontaneous'.

2. School Refusal – After Starting School

If, at some later stage, the child starts refusing to go to school, playing truant, or develops a school phobia – that is, he or she becomes excessively anxious and even physically ill at the thought of having to go to school – then check to see if any of the anxiety sources mentioned above are present. Ask the child's teachers for help when collecting this information but, above all, be observant. However, the child should never get the feeling of being watched as this will only produce additional anxiety. Check discreetly. Watch the child at play to see if any social difficulties are present. Does the child appear very timid when approaching children of the same age? Do they hover on the edge of play groups rather than join in? Are there any signs of bullying, such as unexplained bruises and cuts? Do they have any difficulties, when approaching adults, which might be preventing them from relating to teachers? You should never dismiss any problems as too trivial to bother about. However unimportant they seem to an adult's eyes, even minor difficulties can make the child's life a misery. A specific difficulty – for example, trouble with a bully – can quite quickly generalise so that the whole spectrum of the child's school work suffers.

If there are social difficulties then, as before, you should teach the child how to interact socially. It is not enough just to explain to them what they ought to do. Demonstrate. If there are brothers or sisters, this will make the training easier. Failing that, you and your spouse should role-play other children. Set up some typical situations such as those which take place in the playground, classroom and sports field and teach the child quite directly how to join in a game, share books and toys and deal with rough and tumble at sport. They should also be shown how to handle the kind of name-calling and fun-poking which makes up much of childish conversation. If your child seems especially upset by such 'badinage', he or she should be taught how to laugh at jokes made about themselves rather than become depressed and miserable. They should also be taught how to give as good as they get. All of this can be done in an acting or role-playing situation with the child and will be much more effective if carried out in that way than by simply discussing the problems.

It will also be helpful to look at the level of anxiety in the family, since your child's difficulties may be a reflection of tensions inside the home. The first general problem, which can be translated into a specific anxiety difficulty in the child, is friction between the parents. Research has shown that marital difficulties are quite frequently responsible for school refusal and truancy and we have seen many instances where a child with a supposedly 'school phobia' problem has not wanted to go to school because he or she was worried about what was happening in the home. Many parents either refuse to believe, or prefer not to accept, that their children have excellent insight into, and are very sensitive about, the relationship between their parents. The fact that the father and mother are careful never to row in front of the children is never sufficient to hide the fact that there is antagonism between them. Since the parental relationship is of paramount importance to the young child, any threat to its stability may well cause excessive anxiety, leading to a wish to keep a careful eye on the situation – even though there is little they can do about it.

Another type of generalised family tension, which can lead to a specific difficulty, arises during a period of crisis, when parental attention is diverted away from the child. Such crises could include financial worries; moving house; having another child; or illness. In this case, the stresses on the child may become more complex and include concern on the child's part for the family unit, in addition to lack of attention. Under these circumstances, problems of school refusal, as well as many other problems, such as bedwetting, nightmares, difficult toilet habits and temper tantrums, may occur as attention seeking behaviours. If the child does receive the desired attention as a result of this type of behaviour, even if the response is a scolding or punishing one, the behaviour becomes *positively reinforced* in the way we described in Part One. This can often lead to an increase in the frequency of the behaviour, which will persist even after the crisis has passed.

Clearly, therefore, when attempting to modify a particular problem area for the child, it will be necessary, if family tension is high, to bring these under control at the same time. Marital strategies, which you will find in this Life Area, when used in conjunction with the Anxiety Antidote (which the whole family, including the child, should learn) will enable you to exert this necessary control and reduce the level of tension. At times of crisis, the problem of lack of attention to the child should be rectified by ensuring that there are intervals during each day when the child receives his or her own personal time with the parent/s. Attention should not be given to any inappropriate behaviour which the child is using in an attention seeking way but should follow play or other appropriate behaviour. In this way, desired behaviours on the part of the child will be gradually reinforced and increase in frequency.

STRATEGY THREE

Anxieties – When a Child has a Fantasy Friend or a Fad

There are two main reasons why a child has a fantasy friend. It may be that he or she is lonely, perhaps because of a difficulty in making friends; or because the child is particularly creative and has a vivid imagination. The parental anxiety usually centres on whether the child will grow out of the fantasy friendship and worries that it may be somehow harmful.

Demands for special foods, refusal to eat things and similar fads, create a different type of anxiety problem. They are often very frustrating for the parents, since the 'faddy' child will demand special foods or particular ways of doing things. The anxiety here is usually whether or not the child should be allowed to continue with the fad or if it will be harmful if a stern, 'no nonsense' approach is taken.

Strategies

1. Fantasy Friends: The best approach is not to worry about them. For whatever reason they develop they will not, in themselves, cause the child any problems and will usually be grown out of quite quickly. The fantasy friend can often provide a useful way for the lonely child to gain some way of expressing feelings; and for the imaginative one to develop a creative outlet.

If the fantasy friend is a substitute for other childhood relationships then try to encourage interactions with other children by using the methods described in Strategy Two. Do not try to discourage the fantasy friend, but join in the games in which he or she figures and let the situation work through naturally.

2. Fads: In the case of food fads, it is best to try and gently persuade the child to eat or drink things to which they have taken an inexplicable dislike. This type of fad is often typified by an: 'I don't like it because I haven't tried it' attitude. By encouraging the child to experience as wide a range of foods as possible, you will be broadening their range of options later on in life. The same advice applies to other types of fads, where the child insists on doing something in a particular way or not carrying out certain activities. Fads can be extremely frustrating for parents but you should try to overcome your irritation and adopt a flexible approach to the problem. You may also find that the child will eat or drink something, which they 'dislike' when you offer it, if provided by a relative, friend or neighbour. In this case, you should make use of the situation rather than feel hurt and inadequate. In many cases, a refusal in your presence is an attention seeking behaviour. Let the child develop a taste for the food or drink by allowing them to accept such things from other adults. In time, it is very likely they will accept them from you. The same advice applies to all other types of fad.

STRATEGY FOUR

Anxieties – When Children Wet the Bed

Bedwetting is a fairly common problem. Research has shown that some 14 per cent of all children have a bedwetting problem after the nappy stage has been passed. The parental response is often one of anxiety that their child is in some way abnormal or annoyance that the child is being lazy or deliberately dirty by not waking up and going to the lavatory. The background anxiety which tends to facilitate bedwetting may be due to family tensions and anticipatory anxiety, on going to bed, that bedwetting may occur again. (See also Strategy Two on School Anxieties.)

Strategies

As general training, you can teach the child to wait longer before going to the lavatory during the day, as this helps the bladder to hold more fluid. Antidote training for the whole family, including the child, will lower general anxiety levels in the family. Take the practical step of not allowing a bedtime drink, although this should not be done in such a way that it looks like a punishment. Give the child the drink earlier in the evening so that the bladder can be emptied before going to bed. It is within normal limits for a child to wet the bed up to about six years old and *nocturnal enuresis*, as bedwetting is technically known, should only be regarded as a problem if it continues beyond that age. However, even before this age, the above background habits can be established. If persistent bedwetting occurs after the age of six then the most effective way of treating it is using the buzzer and pad method. But this should ideally be used in conjunction with relaxation training and an investigation of any anxiety difficulties from which the child may be suffering. It is as important to lower or eliminate these anxieties as it is to prevent the bedwetting behaviour itself.

The Buzzer and Pad Method

This mechanism can be obtained from many chemists and child care stores and consists of a buzzer and a pair of gauze pads. One of these pads is fitted beneath a sheet on the child's bed, the other above it, on top of the sheet, so that they are insulated from one another by the material. A second sheet is then spread over the uppermost pad. The pads are connected to the battery-powered buzzer which is placed near the child's bed. If the child wets the bed, the urine completes the circuit between the two pads, and the buzzer sounds. These devices are so sensitive that the buzzer will sound when the very first drop of urine wets the sheet. The purpose is to train the child to wake up on wetting the bed and go to the lavatory. Complaints that the device does not work effectively or fails to stop the problem can almost always be traced to faulty usage. When installed correctly the rate of success is close to 100 per cent.

Watch out for the following key points when using the buzzer and pad system:

(1) Explain to the child exactly how the device works. Demonstrate how to switch off the buzzer and make sure they can control the gadget. They must not become afraid of the equipment and it should never be installed in an atmosphere of punishment or scolding as this will only increase the level of anxiety.

(2) The buzzer control switch should be placed at some distance from the bed so that it is necessary for the child to get up and switch it off. If the switch is placed close to the bed, the child merely reaches over, stops the sound and then falls asleep again.

(3) The buzzer should be arranged so that you can hear the noise. It will be necessary for you to get up to change the

sheets so that the child is rewarded for having gone to the lavatory by getting back into a warm, dry bed.

(4) Reward the child with praise for having got out of bed and gone to the lavatory. If the child is met by an angry parent who grudgingly remakes the bed, it will prevent the device from working effectively.

(5) Be consistent in the use of the buzzer and pad. Use the equipment for several days after the problem seems to have been brought under control. If there is any break in the use of the device, perhaps because you have house guests or leave the child with a baby sitter, the training can be undermined.

When used properly, with the above points satisfied, you should find that the device eliminates the problem in a few nights. But, as we saw earlier, you should also take care to see that any other anxiety-producing difficulties are dealt with. In the older child, relaxation training will be of great help.

STRATEGY FIVE

Anxieties – When Holding Family Conversations

Problems of communication can easily arise in a family where the structure of the day has been very different for each partner. For example, a wife who has been stuck at home with the children may be bored and eager for adult conversation. The husband who has been busy at work may be equally desperate for some peace and quiet. When they meet on his return home, therefore, they have completely opposite needs. This can result in resentments and difficulties which will make it impossible for them to talk to one another effectively at that time and much more difficult for them to communicate during the remainder of the day. Research has shown that the first ten minutes of the return home from work are critical in determining the atmosphere for the rest of the evening.

Other communication difficulties arise when one of the partners is insufficiently assertive about voicing his or her own views and opinions. The anxiety will then probably be due to a fear that the other partner will misunderstand a request, dismiss a demand out of hand or ridicule a point-of-view.

Strategies

Where the problem involves the partners having conflicting needs when they meet at the end of the working day, it is essential to plan for both to have their requirements met. This can best be achieved by setting up a firm contract between them.

1. Making a Contract

This is most effectively done if one partner gives the other what they require and then, immediately afterwards, receives their required behaviour in return. For example, by negotiation the couple may decide that on the husband's return home in the evening the wife enjoys, say, fifteen minutes of conversation, uninterrupted by any other activities. After this, the husband receives his requirements by being left alone for an agreed amount of time so that he can read a paper, watch TV or simply relax. If there are children in the family who are old enough to understand what is happening, they should be taught how to leave their parents alone during the two periods of their parents' personal time. The children can be involved in the contract by being allowed their own time, during which the parents will play and talk with them, uninterrupted by adult pursuits. The periods set aside for each partner could be made more pleasurable, in some cases, by the other carrying out some rewarding piece of behaviour. For example, the husband might help the wife in preparing the evening meal, or the wife might fix the husband a drink or give him a relaxing massage.

The key point of a contract is that it clearly defines who gets what and when. Very often, breakdowns in communication between marriage partners can be traced to ambiguities concerning personal needs, with neither partner being clear whose turn it is to be fulfilled. This type of contract may sound very artificial and unromantic, but is of prime importance to adopt a clear cut ritual in a busy household if the relationship is to remain amicable. Outside these specified personal time periods, life can flow on in a completely unstructured manner.

If anxieties are being caused by a fear of having to voice an opinion or make a request which is likely to prove unpopular, then it is necessary to learn how to make the approach in a more forceful and assertive manner.

2. Assertion Training

Assertive behaviour is not the same as aggressive behaviour. In aggressive behaviour, the aggressor is attempting to beat or score points over the other person. In assertive behaviour, they are simply putting their point of view firmly but leaving the other person with options as to how they might respond. For example, an aggressive exchange might take the following form:

A. 'I am absolutely fed up with this carpet. I insist that you buy me another one.'
B. 'Well you can insist all you like but I wouldn't dream of getting another.'
A. 'That's typical of you and your damned penny pinching attitude.'
An assertive interchange might take the following form:
A. 'Peter, I know things are a bit tight financially right now, but I wonder if we could plan, at some stage, to replace this carpet. Being stuck here all day with it is really getting me down. It would certainly boost my morale if I could see something brighter and more attractive.'
B. 'Well, yes, things are rather difficult at present but if it could wait for two or three months, and after all that would give us time to look, we could probably manage it. Can you wait until then?'
A. 'Yes, that would be great. Just knowing it's coming would help a lot.'

The way is then open for her to start looking for the carpet and for him to start planning financially for it to be bought. In this second interchange, there was more than a demand being made. The wife was showing that she had considered the possible difficulties involved and, although if he had refused she might have pressed her point harder, she was giving him the opportunity to say 'no'. The very fact that he was given the chance to refuse, however, made him feel less cornered. Another aggressive conversation might sound as follows:

A. 'My God, you're home all day with nothing much to do while I'm out sweating my guts to earn the money, and you can't even let me have sex when I need it.'

B. 'Well with that sort of romantic approach what the hell do you expect?'

A. 'Oh yes, any excuse. I suppose that's just more fuel for your fire – or lack of it!'

In this instance, both partners are trying to make each other feel guilty about what they are failing to do for one another. In any such situation, it is only natural to defend an attack which makes us feel guilty, often by making a similar attack ourselves. In this case, the exchange usually deteriorates into a slanging, point scoring row.

The assertive approach here might run as follows:

A. 'Helen, we don't make love as much as we used to and I really miss it . . . is there anything I'm doing that makes it difficult for you?'

B. 'Yes, I am afraid there is. You don't give me those occasional squeezes and kisses like you once did which used to get me all hotted up in the evenings.'

A. 'Really? Hell, the last thing I want to do is start taking you for granted. I can see I will have to put a bit more effort into being romantic. Mind you, it won't take that much effort. . . .'

In this case, the conversation was one which openly asked for and received meaningful information exchange. Points of view were presented quite clearly, but not in any way hurtfully, and the husband was able to use what information was being given to him.

One other thing which you may have noticed in the two examples above is that in the aggressive interchange names were not used, whereas in the assertive one it was quite natural to call the partner by his or her name. This is often the case. In the aggressive or non-communicative situation each party is often referred to as 'you' or simply by implication, through the fact that there is no one else around to hear. It is surprising how much more intimacy enters a conversation when a person's name or some pet name is used. Try it and see.

Use the Antidote to control physical anxiety symptoms and to prevent negative mental attitudes. Ideally, this strategy should be read by both husband and wife. If this is not possible then practise assertive interchanges with a friend. Use mental imagery training in which you go through an exchange with your partner and act in an assertive manner. Watch exchanges between other couples and identify those which are aggressive and those which are constructively assertive. Make use of any tactics, which other couples use in assertive interchanges, that seem effective. When you leave an assertive exchange, debrief on how you managed and what went well. Incorporate these successful tactics into your Positive Self-Talk training sessions.

If anxiety is being caused by your partner constantly failing to meet your expectations or as a result of your self-image being put in jeopardy during these exchanges, then carry out the type of analysis described at the end of Part One. See if your self-image components are realistic. Check out your expectations. Are they based on reasonable assumptions about what you or your partner can achieve or are you pitching them too high? If either partner sets the other up as a paragon of virtue who can do no wrong then disillusionment and anxieties are bound to occur. On the other hand, as explained in Part One, a very negative self-image or negative expectations will produce their own anxieties. Take some time to think about your life objectively and situations which now appear to be a serious source of anxiety may not seem half as important after all.

STRATEGY SIX

Anxieties – When Going Out of Doors

Anxieties caused by leaving the house may be due to a number of difficulties ranging from social problems, such as mixing with other people and fear of criticism; anxiety generated by the problems of somebody close to you – for example, the misery of a school phobic child when being taken to school; or by a phobia, especially agoraphobia. I have provided strategies for some of the other difficulties elsewhere in this Part of the book (see Strategy Two above and Social Anxieties – Strategies Four and Five). Here I want to look at problems relating to agoraphobia, one of the most common phobic difficulties. A recent survey showed that some 89 per cent of agoraphobics are women and that 64 per cent of all agoraphobics developed their problem between the ages of 18–38 years. It is rare in children and seldom occurs after the age of forty.

Agoraphobia is a bewildering and extremely distressing problem because it seems so illogical and produces such intense symptoms of anxiety.

There is a great deal of concealment of their problem, by agoraphobics, from other members of the family, but a high proportion seek medical advice. The same survey suggested that as many as 95 per cent of sufferers went to see their doctor and 75 per cent of these went to seek psychiatric help.

However sympathetic he or she may be, there is not a great deal that the average general practitioner can do, other than prescribe tranquillisers to make the symptoms more bearable. This inability to help is due both to a lack of time and a lack of specialised training in the most effective methods of combating the problem. The most effective method is, without a doubt, the behavioural approach, where a high success rate has been achieved. If you currently suffer from an agoraphobic difficulty you should seek help from a psychologist.

Strategies

Agoraphobia is a complex problem which has wide ranging effects on a person's lifestyle. It is impossible to offer a complete programme for the agoraphobic in the space available here. But here are some pointers towards success:

(1) Carry out your Relaxation, Positive Self-Talk and Anxiety Management training especially carefully.

(2) Go through each situation in your graded list several times, using Mental Imagery before starting to tackle the situation in real life.

(3) When you are attempting the behaviour in real life, remember to use WASP. Agoraphobics will typically hurry through a feared situation with their heads down and minds closed to everything except getting it over and done with as quickly as possible. As explained earlier, such an approach makes it *less* likely that you will be able to combat the anxiety response. WAIT, ABSORB and SLOWLY PROCEED. Use Quick and Differential Relaxation to help you bring down the level of *sympathetic* arousal. Observe your surroundings as carefully and clearly as possible. Walk slowly. Never rush.

(4) After each practical session debrief carefully and congratulate yourself on any successes. Look out for helpful strategies which you used and build them into subsequent Positive Self-Talk statements. For example, you might find that it is easier to travel by bus if at first you sit near the exit. Going into a shop could be less frightening if initially you pick a time of day when it is fairly quiet. You may find that walking down the street is easier if you do it at night. All these tactics can be built into Self-Talk and used to help you through the next training session.

(5) If you do get too anxious then go back to an earlier
situation on the hierarchy list and practise this again on
several occasions before attempting the more difficult
situation. If there are still problems then introduce an
intermediate stage to help you. For example, you might
find that you can cope with crossing busy streets provided
there is no island on which you could become 'trapped'.
But crossing a street with an island proved very anxiety-
producing when there is heavy traffic. The intermediate
stage could be to cross the same street at a very quiet time
of day.

Getting Help

Agoraphobics are quite often helped by members of their
family, but in the wrong way. A sympathetic husband may do
the shopping, take the children to school and refuse party
invitations in the belief that he is helping his wife. But, as you
should by now understand, anything which reduces anxiety
without solving the basic difficulty only serves to reinforce the
avoidance or *escape* response. The husband is actually making
it *more* likely that the phobia will persist by what he intends as
kindly actions.

This does not mean that help should be withdrawn immediately. Such a response would be as misguided as the previous
approach. It will still be necessary for the husband to do the
shopping and take the children to school in the early days of
training. But help should also be offered in carrying out the
Antidote programme. Very often, the presence of a sympathetic
helper will enable the agoraphobic to tackle the situation which
might otherwise have proved impossible. Gradually, though,
collusion in avoidance tactics should be withdrawn as the
sufferer is encouraged to make more and more attempts to carry
out the previously avoided behaviours.

The helper can also assist the training programme by rewarding every attempt with praise. This type of positive reinforcement is very important in sustaining motivation and establishing

the new patterns of behaviour. An agoraphobic who returns home after going down to the shops should be warmly congratulated, even if the attempt has only been a partial success. The phobic who comes home filled with triumph and is met with a sarcastic: 'What's so great about doing that? Anybody with any sense could do it!' is being punished in a most cruel way. However difficult it is for the non-phobic to understand the hell which the phobic is suffering, every attempt must be made. Remember that another person's pain is always hard to imagine and it is all the more difficult if there are no obvious wounds. But the anxiety response which the phobic experiences is very real and very distressing.*

* A tape cassette programme developed especially for agoraphobics has been recorded by Dr Robert Sharpe. For further information write to: LIFESKILLS, 3 Brighton Road, London N2 8JU.

STRATEGY SEVEN

Anxieties – When Over-Dependency Occurs

There are two ways in which an over dependency by one partner on the other can generate anxieties. The first arises as a worry by the stronger partner over what would happen if they became ill, had an incapacitating accident or died.

Secondly, anxiety can be caused by a sense of irritation and frustration over a partner who seems unable to make any decisions or develop any sort of personal life on their own. This kind of unassertive, 'clinging' behaviour often leads to marital breakdown and divorce as the demands become increasingly unbearable.

Strategies

It is clearly better, in a situation like this, for both partners to work on the problem together. It is usually quite unproductive for the more dominant partner to attempt to coerce the dependent partner to 'widen his circle of friends'; 'pass her driving test'; 'cook himself a meal occasionally'; or 'decide where *she* wants to go out for the evening'. By working jointly on the problem, the needs and aspirations of the more dependent partner are taken closely into account.

The first thing which must be done is to establish whether there are any basic and predominating features about the dependent partner's lifestyle which are blocking personal freedom. Do they have a phobic problem? Are they unable to drive and so have difficulty in visiting friends on their own? Are they over-anxious about socialising and making friends? Do they lack the necessary knowledge to do certain things around the house – for example, keep the family accounts or cook a meal? These and similar problems might form an important basis for the dependent partner's behaviour. It is clear that in such cases, action should be taken – by reading the appropriate strategies in this book, for example, or by acquiring the necessary skills in some other way – to rectify the situation.

Of course, the dependent partner may have originally had these skills or possess the ability to acquire them but believe that they could not now achieve these goals. They constantly predict failure if they attempt to carry out any of these skills and see the obstacles as insurmountable. An important method of overcoming this sort of barrier to independence is for the more dominant partner to carry out the behaviour *with* the dependent partner and, by gradually fading from the role of responsible leader in the situation, to encourage the less dominant partner to take more of the initiative. For example, the wife whose dependence has been due largely to having spent several years at home with a young family might, through a little effort on her own account and patient encouragement from her husband, take over a part of his business activities, perhaps by arranging appointments, talking to clients from home or doing book-keeping. From such a beginning may spring her own interest in business and a new career. This may take a lot of doing as far as the more dominant partner is concerned, because while they may complain and protest about the 'burden of taking all the decisions' they could actually prefer this dependency to a more equal relationship. It usually produces a quiet if unstimulating life, bolsters their self-image to be regarded as the 'stronger' of the two, and effectively shackles the dependent partner to the marriage. Although they seldom acknowledge this fact, many men find it less stressful to have their wives at home and away from other 'temptations'.

If there is no support from your partner to break the dependency, this may be because your relationship has adapted to it. Both of you could fear that any radical change to a more independent status might upset the current balance. So when considering if this dependency is a source of anxiety, it is important to ask oneself honestly whether it is really so upsetting or whether you do not really prefer it to the alternatives. If the answer is that you would sooner have dependency than freedom, then learn to live with the situation and stop making it a big issue. If the answer is that you want to diminish the dependency then take practical steps to change your lifestyle. It does not have to be an all-or-nothing change. You may find that the problem resolves itself very well if you and your partner form a contract which gives both of you a limited freedom to do what you want to do independently of the other. For example, you might agree that one partner has an evening a week to go out and socialise or take some spare-time course on their own. In return, the other partner is allowed to follow his or her own activities for a similar amount of time each week. Such a clear cut contract removes many of the niggling difficulties which can surround a less formalised situation.

STRATEGY EIGHT

Anxieties – When Flying

A flying phobia is not an uncommon response. It may arise from a fear of being confined, a fear of heights, a fear resulting from not being in control of the situation or a fear of the aircraft crashing. It is very useful to know which of these, or which combination of them, causes the anxiety, as that feature can then be used when building up a hierarchy of situations to practise. This type of anxiety causes a spin-off problem in family situation as it can cause tension when deciding where and how to go on holiday. Many flying phobics are ashamed to tell even their family of these difficulties and can insist on the holiday being taken in places close to home, or on travelling by alternative forms of transport for reasons which seem illogical to the others concerned.

Strategies

It may help to pin-point which components in air travel make you anxious if you consider, for example, whether you become anxious in other types of confined spaces, such as small rooms; whether you are fearful if you look down from a height; when you are a passenger in a fast car; or if you experience excessive anxiety when you hear about an air crash. If you have been able to fly at other times, remembering at what point you became anxious may also help. Were you more fearful when anticipating the journey than when you were actually in the plane, for instance? Was the moment of take-off more, or less, anxiety-producing than the flight itself?

When you have been able to identify the components of the flight which produce anxiety, prepare a graded list as described in Part Two. Such a list might include:

(1) Talking about our holiday plans.
(2) Buying air tickets and looking at posters in travel agents.
(3) Thinking about the flight the night before.
(4) Travelling to airport.
(5) Waiting in departure lounge.
(6) Moment aircraft door closes.
(7) Listening to engines building up power to take-off.
(8) Looking down from aircraft.

Increasing
Anxiety

Now use these during Mental Imagery training and work through each of them, controlling the anxiety response with Relaxation, until they no longer make you fearful.

During the real life situation, use Quick and Differential Relaxation to help you. Relax in the departure lounge and on the aircraft itself and make full use of Positive Self-Talk statements. During the flight, use a modified form of WASP. Absorb details of your surroundings inside and outside the aircraft which you may previously have been too anxious to observe. Notice how beautiful cloud formations can look, see the way sunlight shafts down onto the banks of white, look at the interesting patterns made by roads, fields and woodland on the ground below. Absorb all these details as fully as you can. Look around the inside of the aircraft as well and take in the general activity. On subsequent trips these details could be incorporated into Positive Self-Talk statements of the kind: 'I know that this will be slightly difficult for me but I will be able to cope more easily if I watch the play of light on the clouds' or 'If I study the work of the air stewardesses.' If the aircraft hits a patch of air turbulence then use the feeling this produces in your stomach as a trigger for Relaxation rather than anxiety.*

* A tape cassette programme developed especially for flying phobics has been recorded by Dr Robert Sharpe. For further information write to: LIFESKILLS, 3 Brighton Road, London N2 8JU.

STRATEGY NINE

Anxieties – When Demonstrating Emotions

An inability to demonstrate strong feelings is often called 'emotional constipation'. The anxiety arises typically when one of the partners starts to complain that he or she is not receiving the required level of response or the desired degree of affection. The tensions caused by an inability to express oneself emotionally can soon spread to other family, social and sexual situations. One common feature of an emotionally constipated relationship is a total absence of any rows. A couple in this situation will report that they *never* have a major argument. Privately they may admit that they would very much like to be able to clear the air and express themselves frankly but they are either frightened or for some other reason unable to do so.

Strategies

In the Emotional Training section of Part Two, we saw that emotions can be trained just like any other pieces of behaviour. When a blockage has occurred, quite drastic measures may be necessary in order to remove it and release the pressure. Surprisingly, perhaps, one of the first steps in helping a couple to express feelings of love for one another may be to help them demonstrate the equally powerful emotion of anger. Once they have learned how to have a good row, they will also be able to indulge much more easily and enjoyably in exchanges during which they put into words and actions their love and affection for one another. The following 'games' have proved especially helpful in removing a block which is restricting all uninhibited expressions of emotions.

1. Exaggerated Anger Training

This group of exercises is fully described in Strategy Six of Social Anxieties. When using them in the marital situation, however, it is vital that at the end of each training session you wind down from the exercise, debrief on how you did and then carry out positive emotional training towards one another in the manner described below.

2. Positive Emotional Training

In these exercises, you should concentrate on building in verbal, non-verbal and intimate touching emotional behaviour.

Verbally, you should spend a few minutes taking it in turn to say what you like about each other. Refer to any aspect of your partner: their appearance, how they smell, taste, and feel, how they talk, what you find fun about them, memories of good times together, their attitudes and achievements. It does not matter if you repeat yourself as each of you takes it in turn simply to tell the other what you find good about them. At the same time, you should touch one another, stroke the hands and face, run your fingers through the other's hair, cuddle and embrace them. When you express yourself verbally and physically, sustain eye-contact with your partner. When all of these activities are put together, you will find it very easy to become quite relaxed and enjoy the situation. If you both want to go on and make love, then do so.

3. Unplanned Arguments and Rows

Take every opportunity to clear the air between you as quickly as possible. Allow angry feelings to emerge in just the same way as when you were using the exaggerated anger playing exercise. Do not choke back the words, but express any resentment or feelings of injustice. Do not be afraid of the outbursts but, when it is over, do not sulk and protract the situation unnecessarily. Start straight away to work on positive emotions and the construction of more appropriate interactions than the one which led up to the row.

In general, do not be afraid of your emotions and remember that you have to practise letting them come out in order for them to do so freely. It is only when they are bottled up and constipated that they will cause you anxiety, so try and release them as quickly as possible.

STRATEGY TEN

Anxieties – When Children Leave Home

Anxieties about children growing away and leaving home frequently arise out of a sense of loss and fear at the vacuum which will be created by their departure. This is quite understandable, as a couple, who may have devoted most of their married life to raising their family, must now construct a different kind of life together without the responsibilities, and the rewards, of looking after their offspring.

Another component of this type of anxiety is often concern over whether or not the child is capable of handling the hazards and problems of life away from home. The worry is likely to be all the greater if the child leaves home at a relatively early age.

Strategies

1. Planning For The Parting

You must not allow the moment of parting to catch you unprepared. Some parents adopt a 'head in the sand' attitude and refuse to consider what life will be like when their children leave. This makes the moment of parting all the more traumatic. Plan for the parting as a family. Do not attempt to conceal your feelings of loss when the child leaves home but at the same time make it clear to the child and to your spouse that you are now entering a new stage in your married life. Many things which were previously impossible, perhaps for financial reasons, should now be attainable. Work on these positive aspects of the changed lifestyle.

Develop a new relationship with your child based on friendship rather than child/parent bonding. It is this bond which the child is implicitly severing when he or she moves away from home. If you try to pretend that it still exists you will quickly sour the relationship. During the period of planning, allow the child increasing responsibility both in what you permit them to do and in accepting the consequences of their own actions.

During this period you should also plan, and discuss as a family, your own futures. By reviewing your possible options as a family unit, you will make it easier for the child to gain his or her independence without a sense of guilt over the inevitable changes which their leaving is imposing on you. A child who leaves home with the sincere good wishes of the parents, having participated in the construction of their new lifestyles, is likely to become a close friend and a frequent visitor. The child who is made to feel wretched and guilty for 'betraying' the parents, by demanding a perfectly justifiable life of their own, is much less likely to want to return on visits.

In most Western cultures, the period of parting tends not to be well defined and this is a pity, since a certain ritualising of the situation can help to make it easier to accept. We could learn a great deal from other societies where the process of 'growing apart' tends to be a formalised affair. Technically this is known as a *rite de passage'* and often involves religious or secular ceremonies designed to mark out the passage from childhood to adulthood, from dependency to an independent state. Try and use the concept of a *'rite de passage'* in your own family. Make something special of the parting. Let the children leave freely and without mutual resentment and they will never be lost to you.

2. Let Them Make Mistakes

Around the time a child starts thinking about leaving home, the parents will often find that nothing they say or do seems to be right. If they try to give advice based on their own experience they will be accused of interfering and making a fuss. If they keep quiet and leave the child to their own devices, they may be told: 'You couldn't care less what happens to me.'

This conflict arises from the opposing needs of the child and the parents. The child wants to assert his or her independence as a young adult. The parents are fearful that the child will make a mistake and this naturally raises anxiety-generating doubts about the future. Will the child fall in with a bad crowd? Will she become pregnant? Will he take drugs?

In these and most other cases, the short answer is that you cannot know what will happen. The best way of dealing with these unknowns is to make sure that the child realises there is always a direct line to the family home if things go wrong. They should also understand that if they have to ask for help it will be given in a non-judgemental way. All too often parents assume that their children will be aware of this. 'She must know we love her. She must know we would want to help,' the parents of a runaway teenage girl protested. Perhaps she did. But it is a bad mistake to believe that people will 'know' anything because you know it yourself. This kind of approach is typified by the: 'I don't have to tell my child I care for him. He should realise I do because I am his father' attitude.

The only way people know how others are likely to respond is from experience of that response. It is important, therefore, to build up this trust well before the parting occurs. Ideally, it will have been constructed through childhood but if there have been difficulties in the past you should make a very determined attempt to resolve them during the period of planning for the departure from home. If advice is sought, give it. But do not preface such help with punishing comments like: 'I told you what would happen . . . why couldn't you have used some sense . . . it's all I could have expected from a child like you.'

Give them the benefits of your experience but do not insist they follow a particular course of action because you want them to do so or because 'it will make mum and dad so unhappy if you refuse'. Such guilt-based restrictions are at best anxiety-generating and, at worst, may cause a drastic reaction against them at a later stage in life.

Letting go and learning to accept a child as an individual with rights and responsibilities is not always an easy piece of behaviour to carry out. Like all behaviours it needs to be practised as frequently as possible. You may well become anxious at doing this but use the Antidote to help control the response.

LIFE AREA FOUR
WORK ANXIETIES AND STRATEGIES

Anxiety Analysis

In order to help you find out which of the strategies in this section are likely to prove the most helpful, read through the thirty statements in the Anxiety Analysis below and note the numbers of any which are applicable to your current difficulties. Then refer to the Answer Chart which will direct you to the appropriate strategies in this and possibly in other Life Areas as well. Where a statement number is quoted against two strategies, make use of both of them, adapting the tactics described to suit your particular requirements.

Anxiety Analysis Inventory

(1) I become anxious if I have to rush a project to meet a deadline.

(2) I become anxious if a subordinate brings a grievance to me.

(3) I become anxious if I have to discipline a subordinate.

(4) I become anxious when asking for promotion.

(5) I become anxious if people ask me to take on extra responsibility.

(6) I am anxious if meetings which I am controlling become aggressive.

(7) I am anxious when my requests at work are not met.

(8) I have become anxious because I have been made redundant.

(9) I become anxious when discussing a part of my company's service with a client.

(10) I become anxious when answering questions at an interview.

(11) I am anxious when waiting to be called in for an interview.

(12) I become anxious with aggressive clients who complain.

(13) I become anxious when the pressure and pace of work increases greatly.

(14) I become anxious if I am asked to do frequent overtime.

(15) I am anxious when I think about retiring from work.

(16) I am anxious when chairing a meeting.

(17) I become anxious if there are frictions between my subordinates.

(18) I become anxious when unfair criticism is made of me at work.

(19) I become anxious when making a presentation to clients.

(20) I become anxious if I am overlooked for interesting jobs at work.

(21) I am anxious when standing up for my rights.

(22) I become anxious and confused in front of an interviewer.

(23) I become anxious and demoralised at the prospect of losing my job.

(24) I become anxious at the thought of my subordinates disliking me.

(25) I am anxious because I have to work to deadlines on most days.

(26) I become anxious if my ideas are turned down at work.

(27) I am anxious when I am given too high a work load.

(28) I become anxious when selling to a difficult customer.

(29) I become anxious if work starts to pile up in a big backlog.

(30) I am anxious if I do not have sufficient time between meetings to prepare.

Answer Chart

Statements Ticked	Most Appropriate Strategies
1, 13, 25, 29, 30	S. One (Work)
5, 14, 27	S. Two (Work) S. Two (Social) S. Four (Social) S. Seven (Social)
4, 20, 21	S. Three (Work) S. One (Social) S. Two (Social) S. Six (Social) S. Seven (Social) S. Nine (Social) S. Five (Family)
7, 18, 26	S. Four (Work) S. One (Social) S. Four (Social)
2, 12	S. Five (Work) S. Five (Family)
10, 11, 22	S. Six (Work) S. One (Social) S. Eight (Social)
8, 15, 23	S. Seven (Work) S. Four (Social)
3, 17, 24	S. Eight (Work) S. Six (Social)
9, 19, 28	S. Nine (Work) S. One (Social) S. Seven (Social) S. Eight (Social) S. Nine (Social)
6, 16, 30	S. Ten (Work) S. One (Social) S. Seven (Social)

STRATEGY ONE

Anxieties – When Working to a Close Deadline

Working to a close deadline can produce anxiety from a number of causes including having to clear a backlog of other work, the stress from people outside who keep demanding to know when and if the deadline will be met, mistake making because of the pressure and having to arrive at decisions and conclusions at a faster than usual pace. All of these anxieties can considerably impair performance and lead to a generally higher level of stress than is normally encountered. The effects of such stress at work can often take a considerable time to disappear and may disrupt other work, social and family activities.

It is important to distinguish between the person who habitually works to a tight deadline, and those who are occasionally called on to alter drastically their normal pace of production when a special crisis arises.

In the first case, those involved will certainly have learned specific procedures and developed practical personal strategies to help them to cope, so far as is possible, with the special demands of their work. However, while they may be able to deal effectively on a day-to-day basis with the ever changing demands made by their deadlines, longer term anxieties can develop. Typically it will be at times when the pressure is no longer on them, such as during holidays or at weekends, that anxiety problems are likely to arise. Such people are often unable to wind down from their time-constrained working existence and may become irritable because they find it hard to structure their free time.

The second type of person is much less likely to have created systems which will enable them to deal with the unexpected deadline in the most effective and least traumatic way possible. Most probably they will have to adapt rapidly their routine methods of working to handle the crisis. This can lead to performance anxiety, especially in people who normally expect to work at a methodical and even pace.

Strategies

. In the case of the person who consistently works to deadlines, it is probably true to say that while at work the level of stress produced by working to deadlines satisfies a need in that person which could not be met in other ways. In my previous book *Thrive on Stress*,* were reported the results of some research which indicated that each person has a different optimum stress level. In order to function efficiently and remain mentally and physically healthy, it is important that we operate at this level. People such as journalists, television personnel, racing drivers, and others who work best against the clock and under stress are usually found to have a high optimum stress level.

The problem here is learning how to change gear, because it is important for the mind and body to experience alterations in pace in order to remain in peak condition. If this is your own problem, we suggest that you learn how to set aside time during both your working and leisure periods so that there is a clearly defined boundary between each. This demarcation line should be made as formal as possible so that there is an actual switching on and off between leisure and work. The time to mark out this boundary may conveniently be the journey between home and work, a shower or bath on return home or a brief period of relaxation during the day to define the boundaries of lunch and coffee breaks. This type of strict compartmentalisation is essential if you are to derive the maximum benefit from either your work or your leisure periods. The boundary setting will have to be a determined and initially quite strictly established activity on your part, since there will always be a tendency for one to encroach on the other. The business telephone call which comes when you are in the middle of your meal or the quick

* *Thrive on Stress.* Souvenir Press.

trip to the travel agents to fix up the family holiday when you are rushing to a meeting; the business papers which you try to read while the family are watching TV and the crossword at which you keep glancing while preparing a report for your firm are common examples of the way in which overflow between two Life Areas can occur.

Decide on a signal which you will give yourself to bring one situation to a close before commencing another. A good method of doing this is to institute a short ceremony, such as changing from work into casual clothes and then having a drink when you get home. In a similar way, such encapsulation can be carried out between each separate task at work. All too often an executive may enter one meeting still concentrating on the details of a previous discussion, so that he or she takes an unnecessarily long time to adjust to the new topics. Instead, the fifteen minutes between the sessions might have been used to relax and wind down from one activity, in preparation for the next. In this way, an effective encapsulation would have been created.

It may seem efficient to work flat out and to take work home but this is a short-sighted and short-term view. The long-term damage in terms of mental and physical illness can be considerable. As the strains on the body become too great, mistakes are likely to be made, leading to further difficulties and a loss of confidence. The man or woman who continually works at high pressure and never learns how to use encapsulation and relaxation to break the pace is treading a precarious tightrope.

The person faced with irregular and unpredictable deadlines who has to pace himself or herself upwards from a methodical routine faces somewhat different problems, although here, too, the ability to encapsulate time into specific periods of work and leisure will be beneficial. The person who is used to being very methodical will often have to forego some of the perfectionistic aspects of having much more time to spare to complete a job. When working to a deadline, it is very often necessary to be expedient, and so less than perfect. There is a good comparison to be drawn between the methods which are most effective when taking an examination and those necessary to work to a deadline. The pace of the effort must be organised within a sensibly structured framework so that one does not arrive at the eleventh hour with only half the necessary tasks completed.

It is best to write out a critical path for yourself with the different sub-goals, which will have to be completed in order to finish the task, noted down against the time each will require to complete. You should set aside additional time to cope with any emergencies, errors and setbacks which are likely to occur. You may subsequently find that this additional time is unnecessary but it is much better to plan for it in advance than discover that your neatly organised programme has to be abandoned at a late stage because of some unforeseen eventuality.

You may also find it helpful to draw arrows between the different sub-goals, as is done by engineers when constructing critical path flow diagrams. Such a physical representation of the actual elements of the task will give you a far clearer understanding of the potential difficulties and problems than simply trying to organise the whole work effort inside your head.

When, and if, things do go wrong, the essential rule is not to panic and abandon your structured programme. This is much less likely to happen if you have predicted such difficulties and allowed for them. Control the physical and mental effects of anxiety using the Antidote. If you are really stuck and find it impossible to concentrate on resolving the unexpected holdups then walk away from your work for five or ten minutes. Take the time out in order to allow your brain to solve the problem away from the probably adverse stimulus control of the work area. Just as you frequently find that you can remember an elusive name, quotation or telephone number when you are *not* thinking about it, so too is it most likely that the answer to a particular difficulty will come to mind when you switch your mind away from an intense concentration on the problem.

When working to a deadline keep distractions to a minimum. Make it clear that you cannot take unnecessary 'phone calls, see visitors or answer queries not directly related to the task in hand. If you try to take on work which is not important, or for which there is no such tight deadline, you will merely be squandering your resources inefficiently.

The same applies to backlogs of routine work which may have built up while working to the particular deadline. You must decide whether or not they form a part of the deadline – in other words, do you have to finish those tasks before you can tackle the time-limited work? If this is the case then the tasks must be included in the deadline sub-goal setting. If not, then plan to work them into your daily routine when the immediate and more urgent business has been completed.

STRATEGY TWO

Anxieties – When Unfair Demands are Made

The anxiety encountered when excessive or unfair demands are made on you may be due to your concern that your colleagues or employers continue to regard you as an enthusiastic and highly motivated member of the work force. They can also be due to a general difficulty on your part in saying 'no' because of the fear that an aggressive situation will ensue or that you will lose the friendship or respect of the person making the demands. Very often, when such excessive demands are made, there is a tendency to try to produce guilt in the other, by pointing out all the negative things which will occur if the demands, or the excuses for not meeting the demands, are rejected. The employer who says: 'Unless you stay behind and complete this work I shall lose the contract . . .' is clearly trying to make the employee feel guilty that by a refusal he, or she, will be letting the firm down. The employee who replies: 'But if I stay behind tonight my wife and children will be very upset that I am late home again . . .', is clearly hoping to establish a feeling of guilt in the employer for suggesting overtime. Such attempts to render the other party guilt-ridden are usually destined to end in a resentful and tense outcome. Those concerned will probably tend to avoid further confrontation and communications between them may begin to break down.

Strategies

If you feel strongly that you are being unfairly prevailed upon to carry out an unusually large amount of work then one of your options, as your absolute right, is to refuse by simply saying: 'No, that will not be possible', without feeling that you have to put forward any justifications for your refusal. It is an invasion of your rights, for a reason to be demanded, and, even if this occurs, you still have the right to say: 'I can see that you are in a difficult position and I feel upset on your behalf. But my answer must remain "no" as it is really not possible for me.' A refusal does not mean that you cannot show your understanding of your colleague's, or employer's, plight and this, especially if accompanied by some helpful advice, may well serve to remove some of the pressure. But if you are persuaded against your will into a resentful agreement, you will be much less likely to try to help on subsequent occasions.

The situation could be a more long-running one, in that you are constantly being asked to do a particular sort of job which you do not like very much. Here, you may not only consider that option of firmly, but politely, refusing, but also of stating your preferences and demanding any rights you may have in the situation. The best method for achieving this will be found in Strategy Three.

'No' is often one of the most difficult words to say. Usually it is hedged around with excuses, apologies, explanations and disclaimers which are intended to defuse what is seen as a very harsh response to a request for help. As I have explained, many of these apologies and excuses are not only necessary but, in anything but the very short term, very damaging to relationships, since they often lead to resentments and feelings of guilt. I have also shown how the blunt 'no' can be softened by the attachment of an empathic and commiserating sentiment which does not detract from the strength of your direct refusal. But even this type of clear-cut rejection of the request requires an assertive approach. This type of response should not be carried out with averted eyes, a 'hang dog' expression or any other indications of guilt. Your body language must be consistent with your words if the delivery is to have maximum effect. You should face your colleague, or employer, squarely and maintain eye-contact while you say, in firm tones, that the unexpected demands cannot, this time, be met. All the procedures can, and should, be practised along the lines described in Strategy Two

(Social). Any criticism which may arise as a result of your refusal to co-operate can be dealt with using the methods described in Strategy Four (Social).

Bear in mind that your first refusal is likely to be the most difficult for you. First of all, you will not have had much practice in exercising your rights to say 'no' without apologising and excusing yourself. Secondly, those making the demands will probably have grown used to your meek acceptance of their requests. Your refusal, especially if couched in the assertive terms we suggest here, is liable to come as a considerable shock. After initial disbelief, the other person may react with either a further attempt to persuade you or irritation that you have decided to stand up for yourself. Whatever tactic they adopt, however, it is essential that you stick to your viewpoint and do not falter. Use Differential or Quick Relaxation and the other Antidote procedures to help you control the effects of anxiety generated by this unfamiliar situation. Stand your ground and exit as quickly as you can from the encounter, using the skills described in Strategy Seven (Social). Remember that to give in so that the situation becomes more relaxed and less anxiety-producing, will be an *avoidance response*. Through the effects of *negative reinforcement*, described in Part One, this will serve to establish the 'giving in to demands' behaviour and make it rather more difficult for you to refuse in the future.

STRATEGY THREE

Anxieties – When 'Demanding Rights'

The anxieties generated by having to stand up for yourself and demand your rights are often associated with the difficulties already discussed in Strategy Two and it is for this reason that they have been linked in the Anxiety Analysis. There are a number of fears which can be produced by the need to stand up for your rights, including a fear of rejection, a fear of aggression and a fear of appearing 'petty minded'. These anxieties effectively establish the other person's viewpoint for them, even when not being deliberately used by them to this end. Many people with this type of anxiety problem are quite capable of 'talking themselves out' of attempting a confrontation or will back down at the first sign of opposition if they do manage to summon up the courage to make a stand. The need to demand your rights can occur in situations where you are receiving a service for money paid, in an interpersonal encounter where there are divergent views and at work where the conditions of employment are inferior to those promised or expected.

I shall concentrate here on the area of work, rather than interpersonal problems. Guidance on these difficulties can be found in Strategy Two (Social); Strategy Six (Social); Strategy Nine (Social) and Strategy Five (Family).

Strategies

Two sorts of situation can arise in which there is a need to stand up for your rights. The first, which can occur in shops, restaurants, when driving your car or travelling on public transport, is the rapidly developing and unexpected confrontation. You may, for example, be faced with poor service, shoddy goods, thoughtlessness on the part of other drivers or a dispute over a seat reservation. In any of these encounters, you will probably have the choice of either accepting the other person's viewpoint and rights as being superior to your own, or assertively disputing them.

The second type of 'right demanding' encounter is one which can be planned for in advance. You know, because of past experience, that under certain conditions, your colleagues or employer will put you in the position of either having to accept something which you consider undesirable or of making an issue out of their demands. In this second sort of situation, it is easier to plan your tactics in advance and rehearse them. Since the basic tactics remain the same for both sorts of 'right demanding' confrontation, I shall start by describing how you can best go about dealing with this more predictable type of encounter.

If you are going to assert your rights successfully and with the least amount of anxiety, it is essential to plan for the confrontation in advance. This will prevent you from putting forward demands which cannot realistically be met or from giving way on points which later turn out to be more vital than they seemed at the time. Decide exactly what you expect to achieve by your demands and focus all your attention on preparing arguments to that end. This may seem an obvious point, yet many people in this sort of encounter allow themselves to be diverted away from the main issues. By sidetracking them, or granting minor concessions on non-essential points, the skilled negotiator can effectively defuse the main demands, however justified. Other people, feeling themselves overwhelmed by the force or content of the opposing arguments, resort to petty goals such as 'giving the person a piece of their mind' or 'telling them exactly what they think of them'. These can be perfectly valid aims in some confrontations but they are most unlikely to further your cause in 'demanding rights' situations. They are most likely either to produce bickering, which is totally unproductive, or to weaken your case, by giving the other person the opening to divert the course of the discussion away from your main point and into an issue over personalities or shortcomings.

If possible, rehearse your arguments with a friend or relative. First have them take the opposing viewpoint and argue as strongly as they can against your case. Then swop roles and argue the case *against* your demands being met, as forcefully as you are able. In this way, you will be able to detect any weaknesses in your own lines of argument, while possibly discovering unforeseen strengths in your opponent's. By this type of preparation, you will not only improve the quality of your arguments but you will also help to remove any anxiety associated with the situation.

The next skill which you should practise is the use of the pause. Many people are frightened by silences during a discussion and rush to fill them with words – almost any words. In Part One, I explained how mental confusion is a symptom of many anxiety attacks. During unexpected confrontations, there is often a surge of anxiety at the start of the encounter which disrupts productive thought. The result is either an incoherent and poorly structured attempt at protest or a rapid exit from the anxiety-producing situation. In the first case, the demands are likely to be rejected because they have been ineffectively presented and in the second the *avoidance response* will make it harder to stand up for your rights on subsequent occasions through *negative reinforcement*, as explained in Part One.

By using the Antidote, you will be able to eliminate the effects of mental and physical anxiety. Relax and bring the level of arousal back under your control. While pausing, consider the situation in an unhurried manner. Such a pause is likely to confuse a protagonist who is not familiar with the Antidote, while giving you time to gather your thoughts and select the most appropriate and forceful kind of argument.

Even with practice and the use of the Antidote you may, of course, fail to have your demands met in full, or even at all. In Strategy Four in this section, I shall explain how you can handle such rejections. The essential thing is not to feel too badly about it. Learn from the failure. Try to discover why you failed by objectively considering the way the confrontation went. Note the tactics used by your opponent to gain the upper hand and incorporate the appropriate counter moves in subsequent rehearsals. Congratulate yourself on having presented your arguments as clearly and strongly as you were able.

Finally, establish as a clear goal your exit from the encounter. It is necessary to recognise when the confrontation is over. This may be at the point where you have gained your demands or where the other person has made a clear and unassailable terminating move. Keep the initiative for breaking off the discussion. When you exit, do so firmly and completely. Even if some bright point occurs to you just after you leave the confrontation, do not go back to make it. Hold it in reserve for future encounters.

STRATEGY FOUR

Anxieties – When Handling Rejections

In learning to assert yourself and either demand rights or make requests, it is important also to learn how to handle the anxiety produced by the inevitable occasional rejections. The anxiety experienced by most people in this situation comes from regarding such a rejection as proving that they are considered generally worthless. Instead of confining the area of the rejection to the particular issue involved, they allow it to spread out so that they start to doubt their ability in all personal interactions.

Strategies

The first action which should be carried out after any sort of rejection or refusal has occurred and an exit has been made from the situation, is that you should debrief yourself on exactly what happened. Go over every word which was spoken while the event is still fresh in your memory and see if you can detect either some fault in your arguments or some previously unconsidered strength in your opponent's.

Avoid destructive criticisms of a general nature concerning your own part in the unsuccessful interaction. Never say things like: 'Well I should have known it would end like this. I always fail. I cannot hope to stand up to a personality as strong as that.' Rather, learn from the encounter and review your performance in a constructive way. What were its strengths and weaknesses? Did you approach the encounter in a timid and half-hearted manner which largely predestined the resulting rejection? Or did you start out strongly, but come to grief at some point in the interaction? If so, where did the rot set in? What was the weakness and how did it come about? Consider, too, your opponent's tactics in securing his or her success. What did they say that was so much more powerful than your own approach? Was it in fact what they said or simply the way they said it? Was it that they stuck to a fairly straightforward, perhaps even simplistic central theme while you allowed yourself to be diverted into side issues which finally made nonsense of your main demands? Was it because they allowed you to do all the talking and dig your own grave with your mouth? Was it more the body language which they employed? Did they remain standing while you were forced to sit down and look up at them? Alternatively, did they sit in a relaxed and non-commital way, perhaps shielded by a desk, while you rose agitatedly and paced the room? If they had an authority which you lacked, how did they demonstrate and capitalise on this authority? Did it derive solely from the trappings of their position, such as a large office or a uniform, or was it mainly a matter of attitude? In the latter case, examine the components which gave them this air of authority and adopt, for your own use, as many as are practicable. In other words, learn from your rejection. Do not try to forget about what has happened as quickly as you can or spend unproductive time reflecting bitterly on your own inadequacies.

Rejections are, in many ways, more beneficial to you than constant successes. Unless you have learned how to extricate yourself from a rejection situation positively, through constructive insight into a number of rejection situations, you may be devastated when eventually and inevitably such a rejection occurs.

Be wary about accepting rejection too soon or too readily. Salesmen are often told that they should only pay attention to the third 'no'. People not used to rejections are often inclined to accept the first 'no' – and back away from the situation. With a little more pressure and coaxing, however, the other person might well be persuaded to adopt a more satisfactory point-of-view. They may indeed *want* to be persuaded but feel the need to put up some token protests.

There are a wide variety of coaxing skills which can be used.

But selecting the best will depend on your ability to read the situation correctly. The four major types of coaxer are:

1. *Empathy:* Allow the person to convince *themselves* of your viewpoint by sympathising with their problems and difficulties while sticking to your demands. Empathic listening skills are more fully described in Strategy One (Social). Basically they involve proving to the other person that you see and understand their point-of-view.

2. *Assertive Persistence:* If the situation is one of some gravity, you may well demonstrate your indignation at the rejection and make your voice and manner even firmer than your earlier attitude. Sustain eye-contact and do not allow yourself to be led away from the main issue. See Strategy Five (Family) for details of assertion training.

3. *Humour:* This is a difficult skill to use and it can quite often appear forced unless handled with sensitivity and timing. A flippant line at the wrong time may lead to a swift rejection. On the other hand, a little tension-defusing humour, especially when the person who is refusing you may possibly lose face or appear foolish by granting your demands, can well give a very constructive escape route by allowing them to seem to be taking the matter too seriously.

4. *Immediate and Unqualified Agreement:* This type of verbal judo again must be handled with 'finesse' and consumate timing if it is not to backfire seriously on you. The skill is *immediately* and *without qualification* to state that, of course, you accept the rejection and feel it entirely justified. This approach usually works only in situations where the other person really does not want to reject your proposals at all and hopes to be persuaded by you to adopt a different course of action. When the carpet is pulled from under their feet by your immediate acceptance of their viewpoint, they may well begin to talk *themselves* into agreeing with your original requests. For example, a sales director approaches his immediate superior with a new and revolutionary marketing concept. He detects a spark of interest

as he outlines the scheme. But when he asks if he might implement it, the actual response is: 'I really don't think it is the sort of thing our company can cope with right now. . . .' Using this strategy the sales director says: 'Yes, I totally understand the difficulties and while I strongly believe in my proposals, I have to agree they are untried. I thought it worth mentioning the ideas but I am not in any way pushing them. I am sure you are right in thinking we should forget all about them.' The likely response, given that spark of interest, is something along the lines: 'Well, I didn't say completely forget them. There are some interesting features and we may be able to think of a way of working them into our current projects.' That is the thin end of the wedge which can then be tapped gently home.

This type of coaxer is unlikely to be effective, however, if used in a sarcastic or exaggerated way.

STRATEGY FIVE

Anxieties – When Dealing with Complaints

This type of anxiety stems from three main causes. First, there is the volume and frequence of complaints. Paradoxically, people who are used to handling a large volume of complaints such as hotel and store managers, usually experience less anxiety than somebody who is only occasionally confronted with a large number of complaints. This is because they not only adopt routine procedures for defusing and dealing with them, but are also able to shield themselves personally from complaints arising out of their work.

The second element in complaints is your ability to do anything about them. If you are in a situation where you are being confronted by complaints about which you can do little or nothing because of your position, then frustration and a feeling of being victimised by circumstances may be a major source of anxiety.

Finally, there is the manner in which complaints are voiced. They may be presented in a constructive and considerate way, in which case the anxiety may well be due to not wishing to offend a reasonable and polite person. Complaints, however justified, which are delivered in an aggressive manner are very likely to produce anxiety in people unused to handling and controlling aggression.

Strategies

The tactics needed to deal successfully with the various types of criticism anxiety vary and will be discussed separately here. In everyday life, however, elements of all three forms of the criticism anxiety components are likely to be present, so that the tactics will need to be blended and adapted to suit your needs at that time. Like all pieces of behaviour, the procedures for handling criticism can only be perfected by practice. If you are in regular receipt of criticisms as a result of your job you will clearly have plenty of opportunity to carry out training in real life situations. If, however, you only occasionally encounter such criticisms, but they cause you great anxiety when they do occur, it may be useful to carry out some practice sessions with a friend or relative in which you take it in turn to deliver and defuse a critical attack.

1. *Dealing with a volume of criticism:* As I explained, practice in handling large quantities of complaints at a professional level soon generates its own strategies for coping in a detached and uninvolved manner. At first, however, there may be a considerable rise in anxiety levels and these are best coped with using the Antidote together with any specialist techniques learned during training. If you are handling criticisms as part of your job, it is important not to allow yourself to lose your temper and reply with rudeness to rude and inconsiderate members of the public or your staff. You may find that holding back your natural desire to respond in kind to rudeness builds up high levels of resentment and frustration. If this anger is not to smoulder or to find an outlet in your private life (it should be mentioned here that the highest incidence of wife beating is to be found in the professional classes who commonly have to take complaints and criticisms from clients and members of the public!), you should expend it in a socially acceptable manner. A strenuous sport is one way of relieving your feelings. But you in turn may also have complaints to make at a higher level in which case you should exercise that outlet to dispel some of your own feelings.

2. *Inability to do anything about complaints:* If you are unable to do anything very effective to deal with the causes of complaints, you are clearly in the unenviable situation of having responsibility without power. The first thing to do is to examine objectively how you came to be in this position in the first place.

If you are being made the scapegoat for the inefficiencies of others, what can you do about it? Are you allowing yourself to be put upon because you feel unable to stand up for your rights at work? In this case, study Strategy Three in this section. Are you being made use of because you cannot bring yourself to refuse requests made by your colleagues or employers? If so, Strategy Two in this section will help you.

It may be, of course, that you cannot avoid the situation. In this case, you must learn how to detach yourself from the critical attack. You should make it clear to the complainant that you are not personally responsible for the problem and, whilst not making excuses based on your lack of power in the situation, you should give a realistic explanation of what it lies in your power to achieve. Do not offer to do anything which it is beyond your ability to provide, in the hope of gaining a temporary respite from the attack. This will most likely only compound the problem at a later date. Make the limits of your responsibilities and ability to be of assistance clear at the outset.

3. *Dealing with rudeness and angry complaints:* Aggressive complaints must be defused as quickly and efficiently as possible, not only to limit the amount of abuse which you have to take, but in order to turn the interchange into as productive a one as is possible.

If you are sitting down when the aggressive complainant comes to see you then rise to match their height. He, or she, will be in a much better position to dominate the encounter if they are able to look down and perhaps lean in towards you in an intimidating manner. When you are confronting them on more equal terms, give eye-contact and say something along these lines: 'I can see that you are very upset. I expect you have reason to be. Let us sit down and discuss the situation.' You should then indicate a chair and sit down yourself. In this way you are 'modelling' a piece of behaviour which they are very likely to imitate.

You should not try to stop them or reduce their outpourings, however aggressive, but rather encourage the flow! This may seem paradoxical in view of our statement that the intention is to defuse the situation and limit the amount of aggression which you have to face. But the fact is that people who are provided with an outlet for their rage and frustrations quickly run out of steam. It is when obstructions are placed in their way that the anger gets stemmed and builds up ready to burst out with even more fury a few moments later. Encourage them to vent all their rage at the same time. Ask questions like: 'Yes, is there anything else you would like to tell me . . . what else happened . . . can you add to that . . . would you care to elaborate on that description . . .?' and so on. When they have expelled their anger in this way, a productive discussion is more likely to be possible.

While listening to all types of complaints, use the Antidote to control anxiety symptoms. By doing so, you will be able to keep your mind clear and reduce such physical symptoms as excessive sweating, trembling and unsteady respiration. These are often difficult signs of anxiety to conceal and one's complainant may well observe and capitalise on them to increase their aggressive approach. The thinking here is: 'I've obviously got him worried. I shall win all my points hands down if I keep on making him sweat.'

Really *listen* to what is being said to you. Do not occupy your mind with thinking up a suitable reply while the other person is still talking. If they are speaking very fast, say you would like to make notes. This will not only indicate to them that you are taking their complaints seriously but it will force them to reduce their pace of delivery to a speed which you can largely determine. It is much harder to be aggressive when speaking slowly than it is when you are able to allow the words to bubble forth in an unhindered stream of comment and criticism. There are three further benefits to be derived from keeping notes. Not only will you clearly establish the points at issue, and so make it easier to comment on them and effect any action which may be necessary to remedy the complaint, but you will also have a record of exactly what the complainant had to say. In this way, it will be far harder for them to come back at a later time with further complaints which they insist were raised during the first discussion. The final bonus gained from a written record is that when the invective and any possible exaggerations have been removed from the comments, the basic criticism may seem, both to you and the complainant, to be really quite trivial after all. If it is a serious and justified complaint, then taking notes will only serve to make this perfectly clear. You are then in a much better position to decide what your next move should be and how urgently the problems will need to be dealt with.

At all times, try and retain the initiative, whether you are inviting them to sit down, encouraging them to expand on their difficulties, persuading them to vent all their anger at one go, or controlling their speed of delivery by the rate at which you are prepared to take notes.

STRATEGY SIX

Anxieties – When Being Interviewed

Anxiety over interviews has a number of closely interconnected components. So far as the external environment is concerned, it is a product of the actual physical size of the interviewing board, the importance of the position for which you are being interviewed and of the attitude, whether friendly, hostile or indifferent of those conducting the interview. Internally, it may be composed of anxieties centred on presenting yourself effectively, negative attitudes generated by a history of failure at interviews, doubts about your competence for the position or a lack of confidence about some aspect of your appearance or personality. All these must be considered separately so far as tactics are concerned, although in the actual situation these tactics will need to be carefully blended together to produce a successful interview technique.

Strategies

Although the external components of an interview, such as the type and size of the board, the attitude of the interviewers and the importance of the job, must be borne in mind, the successful interview technique is a self-orientated one. In other words, you should concentrate on presenting your own personality and skills as powerfully and effectively as possible and not try to adapt yourself to give the interviewers what you *think* they want. It is a bad mistake to answer questions in a way which you believe will please, for example, rather than to allow them to reflect honestly your own opinions and attitudes. Such sycophantic behaviour will be readily apparent to experienced interviewers and is likely to diminish you in their eyes.

This is not to say that certain changes in approach are not

important when it comes to handling various interview situations. For example, you will clearly need to raise the volume of your delivery when answering questions if you are addressing a large board as opposed to a single personnel officer in a small office. But, by and large, the best advice is to concentrate on presenting yourself as honestly and efficiently as possible. The following four basic points should be kept in mind:

(1) Preparation is essential. You should find out all you can about the firm to which you are applying and the exact nature of the post which you hope to fill. Homework in this direction is seldom wasted. You should also anticipate certain commonly occurring questions and prepare answers for them. For example, it is usual for interviewers to conclude a discussion by asking if you would like to put any questions to them. Have a set of questions ready and make them relevant to the job in hand. This may sound like little more than common sense, yet experience of industrial interviewing shows that it is only a minority of candidates who take the trouble to give any thought – let alone real preparation – to the content of the interview.

(2) Use the Antidote to relax you mentally and physically. Allow sufficient time to arrive at the interview without having to rush. Plan for emergencies, like the bus which is late or the sudden absence of taxis on the street. Last minute delays can leave you arriving exhausted and anxious despite your best efforts to relax.

(3) If you have any anxieties about public speaking then read Strategy Eight (Social).

(4) Many professional interviewers are trained to read body language. How you enter and leave the interview room, how you present your answers to questions, the way in which you sit and stand will all speak volumes to the experienced person. If you have difficulty in maintaining eye-contact for even short periods then train yourself in this important skill before an interview. When you are

answering a question, look the person in the eyes as you start to reply and on the conclusion of your remarks. While speaking, however, especially if the answer is a lengthy one, you should look away briefly or eye-contact other members of the board. An eye-contact of more than five or six seconds is not acceptable in Western society, although it is in some cultures, and will lead to feelings of embarrassment and even anxiety on the part of the other person. When carrying out the Differential Relaxation training in the Antidote, you will learn how to move about in a relaxed manner. Make sure you practise this important skill when entering and leaving the interview room. WASP is another important strategy in interview situations, where there is often a tendency to rush through answers in order to get the anxiety-producing situation done with as quickly as possible. As I explained in Part Two, a rash, head down approach increases the level of anxiety and confusion. If you need time to consider your answer then say so and pause for a few moments while you collect your thoughts.

STRATEGY SEVEN

Anxieties – When Retiring or Redundant

Both these situations can generate considerable levels of anxiety which is basically a bereavement type problem. The person concerned mourns for such things as the loss of a structured routine, friends, esteem, a more varied and stimulating life than they are now able to lead, an absence of challenge and opportunity and, of course, a drop in income necessitating other changes in lifestyle which can be equally missed and regretted.

Strategies

Where possible, both these situations should be prepared for. This is almost always possible with retirement and frequently there is some warning, or notice, with redundancy. In the first case, you may have the option of living on a pension without further financial need for paid work. In the latter case, you will probably need, or want, to find alternative employment as rapidly as possible. Although the psychological consequences of both situations may, sometimes, appear rather similar, the tactics needed to deal with them are quite different.

1. Retirement

If possible, you should start to plan for your retirement perhaps as much as five years or more in advance. During this time, you can develop alternative activities to replace work. These may be learning a sport, such as golf, or a skill, such as painting. You might also want to train yourself in some way which will allow you to earn money in a new job after retirement.

It is important to realise that however desirable a life of total idleness may seem when you are under pressure, the periods away from work which you so much enjoy when in full-time work owe much of their desirability to the fact that they provide a sharp contrast to the routines which may make up most of your life. When you are suddenly allowed unlimited access to it, such unstructured freedom can rapidly pall, as there is no longer a much faster and different part of your life with which to compare them.

Variety is not only the spice of life, it is an essential ingredient of mental and physical health and you should plan your retirement in such a way that no one thing dominates it. A sport, however much you enjoy it, can only offer a finite amount of challenge and variation. A hobby, if followed without any other distraction, can only rarely produce sufficient stimulation to keep you happy for what may be two decades, or more, of life.

Find a number of things you like to do. Train in some of them while at work, so that you will have activities, in which you possess a good level of skill, ready for you as soon as you retire. Others can be left to develop during retirement but you should bear in mind that the reduction in income normally associated with retirement may make it hard to follow high cost leisure activities after you leave work. Subjects and pursuits which can be learned without much equipment and without the need to belong to expensive clubs, or follow costly training programmes, can be left to retirement. Others should be prepared for, both from the point-of-view of training and purchasing the equipment, while the level of income is at its highest.

Many people are tempted on retirement to move to the coast, the country or warmer climates. This can be an excellent idea but it requires a great deal of planning. All too often, a couple in retirement find that they have exchanged friends and familiar neighbourhood for a possibly healthier, but far lonelier, existence cut off from all their old neighbours. Unless they are prepared to make a determined and active effort to build up new friendships, they may become increasingly isolated and depressed.

In Strategy Six (Sexual) I mentioned the concept of ageism and the attitude that there are certain things which people beyond a certain age should not do. Do not let social prejudice prevent you from taking up a sport or leisure pursuit which you want to follow. Provided you are in good physical health, for example, there is no reason why you should not take up activities which are typically regarded as 'young people's' pursuits, such as sailing, flying, horse riding, running or swimming. People of sixty and more have tackled all these pursuits, and many other equally strenuous ones, with a great degree of enjoyment and success.

2. Redundancy

In addition to the anxieties created by the loss of employment which I discussed above, redundancy, as opposed to retirement, often includes a strong element of rejection. The person made redundant may feel, perhaps with justification, that they have been unfairly singled out. Why should they have been cast aside when others in the firm were kept on? However potent the economic arguments offered to explain a particular redundancy, it is hard for the individual not to view the fact of dismissal as a personal slight and reflection of their inadequacies in some direction.

When applying for other jobs, it is necessary not to do so while nurturing the resentment produced by these understandable but unproductive feelings. First of all, do not allow the redundancy to generate negative thoughts and predictions about your performance at future interviews. Try to adopt an objective attitude towards your redundancy. This is not to say you should simply shrug your shoulders and accept it with a fatalistic philosophy. But you should try to step back from the situation to see whether there are any personal reasons why you, rather than some other employee, was selected for redundancy. There may be clear economic or internal structural reasons, the decline in demand for a particular product or service, the need to close down a whole department which is no longer viable, for example. There may also be personal elements involved, such as the dislike for you by a member of the management. The point is that none of these should prejudice your getting further employment. On the other hand, if you can manage a sufficiently objective appraisal of the situation, you may find that you did contribute towards your own redundancy. Perhaps your level of work had fallen off in recent months or you were having interpersonal difficulties with your colleagues, for which, if you are honest with yourself, you will accept some of the blame. In Strategy Four in this section, where I discussed, in detail, ways of handling rejections, I mentioned the need to extract productive information from any type of rejection. This same advice applies to this situation. Try to learn from what has happened and make use of the newly gained information in the future. It will also be helpful to read Strategy Four (Social), where I discuss how to deal with both fair and unfair criticism.

STRATEGY EIGHT

Anxieties – When Disciplining Subordinates

Anxiety here may be produced by a concern that the employee whom you are disciplining might subsequently think badly of you or that they may become malicious after being disciplined and cause trouble in areas of industry and commerce where militant action is common. In such situations, extreme caution may well seem to be indicated.

A further anxiety source may relate to the manner and location of your disciplining behaviour which you may not know how to do in the most effective and acceptable way.

Strategies

When disciplining subordinates, it is important to refrain from either personal invective or sarcasm aimed at undermining self-confidence and morale. The use of such tactics is not only an ineffective means of making your views known but it may also generate a quite reasonable sense of grievance in those at the receiving end.

The first thing is to be clear in your own mind what you want to achieve by exercising your authority. There is an old saying that talking without thinking is like shooting without aiming. Quite frequently, an ill-considered piece of disciplining can trigger off a serious piece of industrial action which leads to consequences out of all proportion to the original fault. This is not to say a person in authority should hesitate to exercise their rights to insist that work is done in accordance with the needs and regulations of the company. But it does mean that care and skill are required in the disciplining of any subordinate.

Ask yourself what you want to get out of the encounter. Is it to increase a low level of production, to prevent a mistake from happening again, to improve bad time-keeping or what? Set out the cause of complaint as factually, clearly and politely as possible. Having done so, ask for information so that the subordinate has a chance to explain how a particular problem has arisen. There is nothing more frustrating for a person who is receiving a dressing down than being unable to mention some possibly very simple fact which can explain the whole situation. When giving the person a chance to speak, do not rush them. Remember, they will just have been shaken by experiencing direct criticism. Offer a cigarette or a coffee to defuse the situation and allow them to speak at their own pace. Do not try to put words into their mouths.

There is no reason why, if you feel angry, you should not indicate that anger to them in clear terms. But do not carry out the disciplining when you are so furious that you cannot control your responses. Let the initial surge of rage die down before entering into the confrontation. Then use the assertive approach discussed in Strategy Five (Family). Remember that assertion is an act of defending your own rights and position, which is both justifiable and productive, while aggression, the normal by-product of intense anger, is the attempted demolition of another person's position. This is not only undesirable but extremely counter-productive.

Finally, a word about the right place for such disciplining. This should never be carried out in front of the subordinate's friends and colleagues as it may result in an unnecessary resentment, producing embarrassment all round. Respect for your subordinate's rights to fair treatment and privacy, and, providing it was justified in the first place, a dressing down, however severe, should not lead to any ill-will in the future.

STRATEGY NINE

Anxieties – When Selling

Selling yourself, your ideas or your goods in the most effective way is a highly skilled business which requires practice and the knowledge of important basic interpersonal skills in order to be perfect. Most of the anxiety generated by selling arises from a fear of rejection, which is discussed at length in Strategy Four in this section. However, part of the anxiety may also be due to not knowing how to pace a sales pitch effectively. It is with the skills necessary for effective pacing that we are concerned below.

Strategies

Three basic skills, which can receive any number of personalised embellishments once they have been mastered, are necessary in any selling situation. These are:

1. *Empathic listening,* which you can use to get under the skin of your client. This skill has been described in Strategy One (Social).
2. *Assertive sending,* which is also described in Strategy One (Social).
3. *Effective exit or closure skills,* when a deal has been struck.

These are described in Strategy One (Social) and Strategy Seven (Social). You should read all these strategies and make sure that you fully understand the principles involved before starting to use them in the sales arena.

The first goal which you wish to achieve is the trust and respect of your sales prospect. Listen attentively and use empathic responses in order to get them saying such things as: 'Yes, I can see you really understand my needs in this area.'

During the execution of this goal do not attempt, too early, to push alternatives in front of them. When you are confident that the person trusts you, establish the next goal which is the presentation of your goods or services. You can do this easily and naturally by saying that you believe that among your particular range of products or services there are some which could meet the stated requirements. Go on to describe them concisely and interestingly so as not to become boring and repetitive. When the prospect has narrowed down the field to a specific service or commodity, you should then start using the third skill of closing the deal, with the assurance that it will go through.

When stated like this, these three stages may seem obvious. Yet we often find that, for example, the first stage is left out in an eagerness to put the product or service on display or the exit is bungled and the deal left uncompleted. By breaking the business of selling down into its basic components in this way, it becomes possible to practise and perfect each of them separately. They can then be put together with the time spent on each and the pace at which each of the three is completed varied according to the nature of the sales pitch and any problems which crop up during the interaction. For instance, if difficulties arise during the closing stage it may be necessary to revert to the first skill of empathic listening in order to regain the client's confidence. When correctly blended and paced, these three skills form a most potent mixture and, all other things being equal, should ensure sales success.

STRATEGY TEN

Anxieties – When Managing Meetings

A number of skills are needed to be an effective chairman and anxieties which arise when managing meetings are usually due to one or more of the following: inadequate preparation which allows others to take advantage of your lack of knowledge of the topic being discussed or the rules of that particular meeting; an inability to keep the discussion on the main topics before the meeting; a failure to keep proper records; a lack of control over personal frictions between those attending the meeting.

Strategies

Let us start by making three general points which will be well known to any readers experienced in managing meetings but which seem to be frequently forgotten by those who only occasionally have to take charge of a formal discussion. The first concerns adequate preparation. Before taking charge of any meeting, you must ensure that you are familiar with all the relevant information and that you have, as far as possible, summarised any major points of disagreement and discussion which others at the meeting may produce. These preparatory notes should be set down neatly and, if possible, circulated among members attending the meeting before it occurs. This will give those taking part a reasonable amount of time to consider how they are going both to introduce their own ideas and deal with points raised by their colleagues.

The second skill which needs to be perfected is keeping the meeting on the topics detailed on the agenda. You should make strenuous efforts to prevent extraneous discussions developing when going through the agenda, as, while this may be acceptable to members who have come along for a general discussion, i will be disrupting to those who wish to discuss specific topics General discussions should always be confined to the 'any othe business' section of the meeting.

Finally, notes which can be used at later meetings should b kept after each salient point is discussed and agreed upon Often, in small business concerns, the chairman will fee confident that he, or she, can remember the details of shor meetings. But invariably these recollections are either forgotten or even more damagingly, on occasions, incorrectly recalled The Chinese proverb which states that: 'The palest ink i brighter than the brightest memory' should be taken very much to heart.

One skill which is often lacking, even in those who have frequently chaired meetings, is an ability to reduce friction and handle the interpersonal relationships involved in such a way that the more aggressive or articulate members are prevented from dominating proceedings at the expense of equally deserv ing but less dominant members of the group.

The wise chairman knows as much as possible about the personality and debating styles of those attending his meetings He, or she, should be able to decide quite easily who will need a degree of regulation and who will need to be drawn into the discussions and encouraged to state their views.

Where the seating around the meeting table is under the chairman's control, rather than being dictated by the status of those attending, it is often helpful to seat members according to their likely level of dominance.

The first rule is to prevent two or more dominant members sitting beside one another. It is also helpful to position them in such a way that you can easily give them direct eye-contact. This means either facing you across the table, or at an intermediate distance to the side of you. If they are seated too close you may have to turn uncomfortably to apply eye-contact; if they are too far away then they may not be able to read your body language signals so clearly.

One should also consider the distance between the chairs on which the members of the group sit. Often these distances will be dictated by the size of the meeting room. But where space is available, the chairs should be spaced out so that each member has at least eighteen inches on either side. This has two effects. First of all, research has shown that we each have a 'personal space' surrounding us. Any intrusion into this area is seen as a threat and while it may not be recognised as such, is likely to generate discomfort and some anxiety. You can easily prove this by reducing the distance between yourself and a colleague during a formal business discussion. At a certain point, you will both become uncomfortable and it is very likely that if you stand your ground, the other person will back off so as to increase the distance and re-establish his, or her, 'personal space'. A second advantage is that collusion or friction between members of the group is less likely.

If personal frictions do occur, it is up to the chairman to stop these at an early stage by carrying out a task-orientated skill such as stating firmly that outside matters should be discussed elsewhere and it is necessary to continue with the main business of the meeting.

A very important meeting skill is 'time allocation'. This relates to all of the above skills and involves, particularly during the preparation stage, deciding which items on the agenda are of primary importance and need more time for discussion and which are trivial and can be quickly disposed of. For example, production difficulties on a tight deadline order might well be allocated half an hour of discussion, while exploring details of a project which will not come to fruition for several more months should be restricted. All too often, in the enthusiasm which a new project produces, this time allocation can be reversed unless a careful control is kept.

A good chairman must be assertive so that his, or her, authority is sufficient to control the meeting from first to last. Only where such effective control is present can a fully productive use of the time available be assured. The skills needed to behave in an assertive manner can be found in Strategy One (Social) and Strategy Seven (Social).

Some anxiety may also be generated by having to speak to the meeting. This difficulty is discussed in Strategy One (Social).

LifeSkills

A practical series of tape cassette programmes
and books designed to help you handle
a wide range of stressful situations in life.

Brighton Road, London N2 8JU

ANXIETY AND STRESS MANAGEMENT
AUDIO CASSETTES

These tape cassettes have been in widespread use amongst doctors, hospitals and universities over the last twenty years. They are presented by behavioural psychologist Dr Robert Sharpe, under whose direction they were developed. They are clear and highly practical in their content and their duration ranges between 45 and 65 minutes.

Relax – and Enjoy It!
A complete course in deep, quick and differential relaxation. These techniques provide the basis for anxiety management training, overcoming phobias, reduction of tension and fatigue and good eating and sleep habits.

Control Your Tension!
This cassette follows on from 'Relax – and Enjoy it!' which should be practised first. The user is taught how to detect and use an anxiety surge as a trigger for quick relaxation and positive mental strategy building. This is of particular value to those involved in stressful occupations or phobia and anxiety sufferers.

Sleep Well!
Mental turmoil and physical tension are often jointly responsible for insomnia. The course teaches how to prepare for effective sleep by using techniques which get rid of worries before going to bed and getting the body in a relaxed state ready for restful sleep. Where anxiety is a particular problem, this cassette should be used in conjunction with 'Relax – and Enjoy It!'

Assert Yourself!
This course teaches three types of technique: conversation management; skills for self presentation and stating your case clearly; and self protective techniques for handling unwelcome pressure from others. Techniques for rapid analysis of interactions are also taught.

Don't Be Shy!
This course deals with starting and developing relationships. Conversation skills, dealing with rejection, entrance and exit skills for joining and leaving groups, choosing the meeting place and deepening the closeness of a relationship are all dealt with in a practical way.

Do Well in Interviews!
This teaches the principles of interview technique for use in all kinds of job application. 'Right-way-wrong-way' illustrations are combined with an 'answer-back' technique where the user can practise while the tape is playing.

Study Effectively!
This course teaches study habits for the student at secondary or tertiary level. Time scheduling, work routines, term and year planning, note planning, ideograms (fact and concept diagrams), rapid reading, good sleeping habits, dealing with backlogs and self-motivation are covered.

Pass That Exam!
For the same type of student as 'Study Effectively!', this course teaches the examination techniques of preparing revision notes, memory training, exam paper analysis, choosing questions, time allocation, answer construction, dealing with 'getting stuck', relaxation and briefing skills for before the exam and debriefing skills for afterwards.

Beat Agoraphobia!
This is a 'question-and-answer' cassette very relevant to the agoraphobia sufferer and their family. Used with 'Relax – and Enjoy It!', this cassette provides a wealth of valuable and practical methods of overcoming agoraphobia.

Fly Without Fear!
This course, best used with 'Relax – and Enjoy It!' and 'Control Your Tension!', uses realistic air travel sound effects and a special series of instructions to control the fear of flying.

Control Thunder Phobia!
Again to be used with 'Relax – and Enjoy It!' and 'Control Your Tension!', this course uses thunder sound effects and a special series of instructions to control thunder phobia.

Think Thin!
This provides a comprehensive psychological approach to dieting and slimming. Techniques are taught for improving self-image, learning 'thin-eating' behaviour, overcoming cravings, controlling 'binge eating', learning to say 'no' and remaining calm and relaxed whilst dieting. Twenty rules for developing alternatives to overeating are also taught.

Kick the Smoking Habit!
Techniques for controlling the smoking 'triggers' in the environment are taught in this course. The user is then shown how to benefit from the payoffs of stopping smoking, motivate themselves to stay on the programme, build up a new 'non-smoking' self-image, develop self-assertion in refusing cigarettes and overcome the craving for tobacco.

Please write for details of cost to the address on page 261.